£1.50

Alan Russell

# RECORD BREAKERS

British Broadcasting Corporation

For Anieka

All records have been checked
up to the time of going to press
in July 1976

Published by the
British Broadcasting Corporation
35 Marylebone High Street
London W1M 4AA

ISBN 0 563 17195 2

First published 1976
© British Broadcasting Corporation 1976

Printed in England
by Hollen Street Press Limited
at Slough, Berkshire

# CONTENTS

# DID YOU KNOW...

. . . that if you shouted "Sail Ho !" on the Pacific island of Pitcairn when there wasn't a boat in sight, you'd be fined twenty-five pence, or get one day's hard labour on the public roads, or be made to fashion a wooden oar for the public boat !

. . . that in October 1964, after a performance of the ballet "Swan Lake" in Austria, Margot Fonteyn and Rudolph Nureyev took eighty-nine curtain calls !

. . . that St John's Lane in Rome, Italy, is only forty-eight centimetres (19 inches) wide ? That's just eighty-nine millimetres (3½ inches) wider than this open book !

. . . that the Hoang typewriter, with 5,850 different Chinese characters, is the slowest and most complex typewriter in the world !

. . . that Richard Dodd returned a book to the Cincinnati Medical Library on 7 December 1968 that had been borrowed by his great grandfather in 1823 – and that the £9,435 fine was waived !

. . . that the Sheffield Wool Shear Workers' Trade Union only has nineteen members !

# JUST FOR THE RECORD

Roy Castle asks the questions. Norris McWhirter, Editor of the Guinness Book of Records, supplies the answers.

**Roy** What is a record?

**Norris** A record is something measurable which represents the extreme of either inanimate objects, such as the highest mountain, or that which has been achieved by the human race. It is measured by the stop watch, measuring tape, weighing-scale, or in terms of frequency – the number of times somebody has done something.
Records can be absolute or qualified. For instance, the fastest speed at which any human has travelled – the absolute record – is over 24,000 miles per hour. This was set over seventy-five miles above the earth's surface in space. But you can qualify the human speed record, by limiting it, for instance, to the speed record on land, or on water, or in the atmosphere, as opposed to the absolute record.

**Roy** Why do we have records?

**Norris** Records, like those any company keeps, are very often a measure of progress, although of course, in some activities, they are a measure of the opposite, such as the greatest number of forest fires started by careless humans with cigarettes. But when it comes to the chronicling of records, there's a great attraction because they represent the extreme, the latest word, the furthest the frontier has been pushed.

**Roy** When were records first catalogued?

**Norris** The earliest records in existence are on clay tablets, from the Sumarian civilisation in the fourth millennium BC, which were tallies kept for the output of mines. The oldest record of an achievement which has survived is probably that of St Daniel the Stylite, a religious fanatic who lived on top of a stone pillar in Syria for more than thirty years. His record, set some seventeen centuries ago, still stands.

**Roy** When did you first become interested in records?

**Norris** In common with a lot of other boys, it was round about my eighth birthday, when I began being impressed by the fact that one ocean liner had more funnels than another, another was longer, another heavier and another faster. I started to make lists of ships, then of mountains and then of rivers, and in this way developed an interest in what was at the top of the list as opposed to those which were further down.

**Roy** And how did you take it up as a career?

**Norris** One day a famous breakfast food company asked my brother and me for a series of twelve record breakers and I remember that in the first one we chronicled the man who'd won the most Victoria Crosses. We found that there were three people who had won the Victoria Cross twice, and the one that we chronicled was the first of these, Colonel Martin-Leake who lived near Hatfield in Hertfordshire.

**Roy** How many different types of record are there?

**Norris** We chronicle, annually, about fifteen thousand different records, and one of the astounding things is that between four thousand five hundred and five thousand of these change each year, about a third of them.

**Roy** Out of the thousands of records you've known during your life, what is your own personal favourite?

**Norris** If one is forced to say which of all the many records one regards as the most significant, then certainly the one on which more care, more man-power and more money has been lavished than any other, is the first human to step on the surface of the moon. Neil Alden Armstrong took off from Cape Kennedy in Apollo XI, on 16 July 1969, and landed 5 days later on 21 July. It was a culmination of the United States Space programme which, at its peak, employed three hundred and seventy-six thousand people and which has been estimated to have cost, up till then, twenty-five thousand million dollars.

**Roy** What about the ones you've personally witnessed?

**Norris** I've had the opportunity of witnessing a considerable number of records, in some sixty-two countries, but the ones that really live most vividly in the memory are those in which one's been personally implicated, not purely as a spectator but also, to some extent, as a participant. Of these, the one which I recall with the greatest interest and affection, was the first four-minute mile, run by Roger Bannister on 6 May 1954. The circumstances behind it really made it a sensation, because there was a real belief that there was some magic about the four-minute mile as a barrier.

**Roy** Are there any other record barriers you're particularly expecting to be broken?

**Norris** Yes, lots. Round numbers have a great attraction in record breaking, and there are several that could be reached in the foreseeable future. An eight-foot high jump, a twenty-foot pole vault and an eighty-foot shot putt are all possible. I believe it won't be too long before we see 600 lbs above the head in weight-lifting. These barriers all exist and are probably within the compass of human physiology.

I'd also like to see centenarian triplets, and I'd like to see a comet even more spectacular than Halley's. That could happen at any time – but the odds are against it. I'd like to see the sound barrier broken by a car – and that's something that could happen sooner than most people think.

Roy   Is there any end to record breaking?

Norris   Well, yes. Records, which have to be measurable and which are always quantitative, will be broken by smaller and smaller margins at longer and longer intervals, getting closer and closer to the ultimate in record breaking but never quite reaching it. The shearing strength of bone is the limiting factor in weightlifting, for example, and a fraction of a gram beneath that is the ultimate for that record. But there's a long way to go yet. At the moment most records are so perishable that even a newspaper, let alone a book like this, can print something that's a record, only to find by the time it gets to its readers, the record's been broken.

The world's tallest tree grows another foot, the longest moustache in the world grows another inch, so although you think you've established the record with the tree, or the face which is carrying the moustache, the actual record keeps on changing, and that's why the business of updating and amending records is always an arduous one.

Roy   What about you, Norris, is there any record you'd like to break?

Norris   Yes Roy – one. I would like to visit each of the one thousand and forty satellite islands around Great Britain. It's something I've always wanted to do . . .

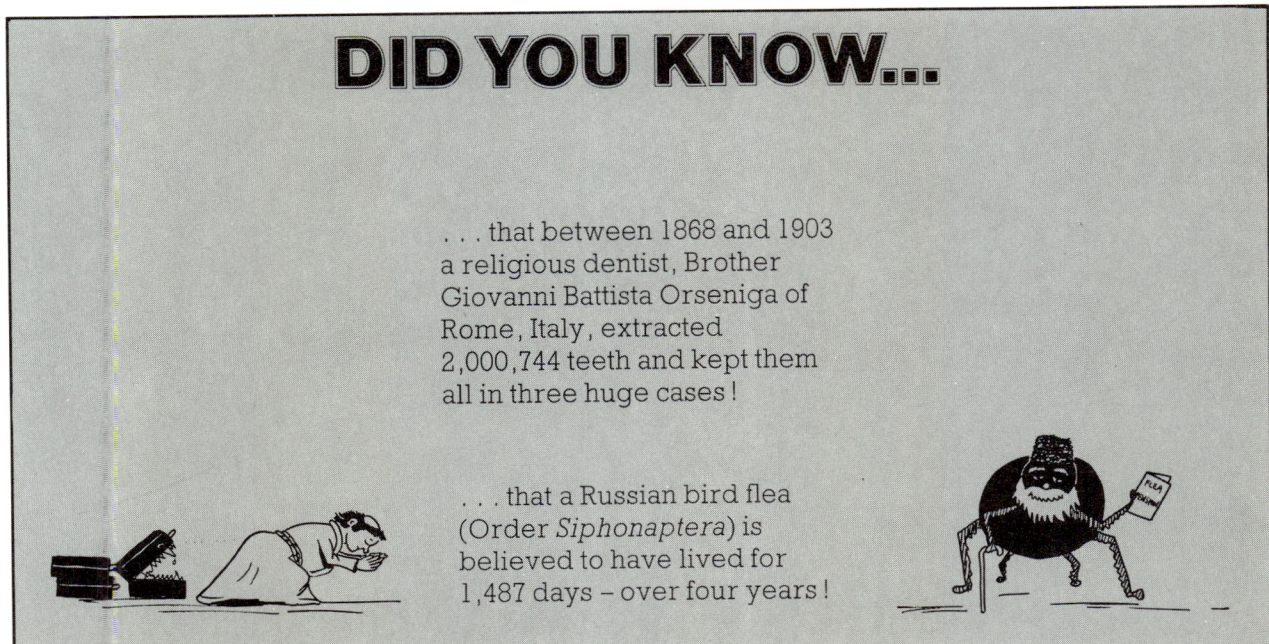

# DID YOU KNOW...

. . . that between 1868 and 1903 a religious dentist, Brother Giovanni Battista Orseniga of Rome, Italy, extracted 2,000,744 teeth and kept them all in three huge cases!

. . . that a Russian bird flea (Order *Siphonaptera*) is believed to have lived for 1,487 days – over four years!

# THE BIGGEST OF THEM ALL

On 25 June 1975 Jim Sparks climbed up a tree. He climbed down from it on 25 August after eight weeks, five days, twenty-one hours and fifty-six minutes. It's the longest time that anyone has remained up a tree, and he's a sore sap-sitting Record Breaker!

He performed the feat in California, the American state famous for its trees, and which holds nearly all the tree records.

Near the White Mountains in the Inyo National Forest on the east side of California, three thousand and fifty metres (ten thousand feet) above sea-level, is a Bristlecone Pine named Methuselah. It's been

there for the past 4,600 years and is believed to be earth's oldest living thing.

In March 1974, it was reported that Methuselah had produced forty-eight live seedlings, so even if the grand old man of trees died today, there are still forty-eight "Methuselah Juniors" to keep us going for another four thousand odd years.

The reason Bristlecone Pines live so long is that they grow in desert areas that have hardly any rainfall. Their growth-rate therefore is exceedingly slow. So too is their death, because wood doesn't rot in a desert, not even dead wood.

Methuselah

Not all California has a desert atmosphere, however. Along the Pacific coast on the west side of the state is a narrow fog belt, where the ocean mists roll in during the summer and as much as two thousand five hundred and forty mm. (one hundred inches) of rain can fall in winter. It's there, in Redwood Creek Grove in Humbolt County, that a tree called the Howard Libbey has grown. And it's grown and grown and grown to a height of one hundred and eleven point six metres (three hundred and sixty-six point two feet) – that's twice the height of Nelson's column. It's the tallest tree in the world.

The Howard Libbey is a Coast Redwood or, to give its botanical name, a *Sequoia sempervirens*.

The Coast Redwood was named "Sequoia" in 1847 by the Austrian botanist Stephen Endlicher. An eminent linguist, he derived the name from a half-blooded Cherokee Indian called Sequoya, who had died a few years earlier.

Reputedly the son of an English trader, Sequoya was born in a village on the Tennessee river in the 1760s and brought up by his Indian mother. Like many Indians at that time, he never learned to speak, read or write English. But he recognised one of the secrets of the white man's superior power, a written language, and systematically set about developing one for the Cherokees. Over ten years later, in 1821, after adapting letters from English, Greek and Hebrew books, he had perfected a new alphabet of eighty-six letters, representing all the

syllables of the spoken Cherokee language. The system was simple and ingenious enough for most pupils, including his own daughter, to learn it rapidly. Books and newspapers were published in it, and schools were established to teach it. Cherokees could now read and write their own language because of Sequoya, the only man in history known to have invented an entire alphabet. While the Indians discovered their new written language in the east of the country, white men were making other discoveries in the west.

In 1833, a party of explorers led by Lieutenant Joseph R. Walker crossed the Sierra Nevada mountains from the east into California. On the descent into a great valley, members of the expedition came across a grove of giant red trees.

Unfortunately, the stories they told about them on their return home were met with disbelief and it wasn't until 1852 that a hunter called A. T. Dowd accidentally stumbled upon them again. He was following a wounded bear at the time. Only after *his* discovery did news of the giants reach the east coast and Europe. Botanists from all over the country longed for samples in order to be the first to describe the new species, but it was an Englishman, John Lindley, who first succeeded. He received cones, foliage and wood samples of the monster from William Lobb, another Englishman who had just returned from a trip to California. Lindley called the species *Wellingtonia gigantea*

The Howard Libbey

11

in honour of the Duke of Wellington. The following year, 1854, the French botanist Joseph Decaisne, recognised it as a species of Sequoia and called it *Sequoia gigantea*. Back in America, other people patriotically called it *Sequoia washingtonia*.

With the row about the naming of the botanical giants still going on, a pioneer by the name of Hale D. Tharp settled on the Kaweah river to raise cattle. He became friendly with a tribe of the Monache Indians and while on a trip to visit their lands in the mountains in 1858 he came across a forest of the enormous trees – a giant forest. Tharp was so impressed with the size and mystical beauty of the trees that he built himself a summer home in a hollow log in the forest.

Twenty-one years later a hunter called James Wolverton made that log his home – the Giant Forest's first permanent resident.

On 7 August 1879, Wolverton, on one of his hunting trips deep in the forest, came upon a *Sequoia gigantea* that was even bigger than any others he had seen – the giant of giants. He named the tree "General Sherman" in honour of the man under whom he served as a first lieutenant in the American Civil War.

Roy Castle at the base of the General Sherman. The photograph of the whole tree makes it almost impossible to see him.

James Wolverton had discovered the most massive living thing on the face of the earth.
Its vital statistics are as follows:
Height 83.00 metres (272.4 feet)
Base circumference 30.96 metres (101.6 feet)
Base diameter 11.14 metres (36.5 feet)
Diameter 18.28 metres (60 feet) above ground
  5.33 metres (17.5 feet)
Diameter 36.57 metres (120 feet) above ground
  5.18 metres (17.0 feet)
Diameter 54.86 metres (180 feet) above ground
  4.26 metres (14.0 feet)
Weight of trunk (approximately) 635 tonnes (625 tons)
Total volume of trunk 14,16.18 cubic metres (50,010 cubic feet)
True girth measured at 1.37 metres (4.5 feet) above the ground
  24.11 metres (79.1 feet)

If the above doesn't convey the massiveness of the General Sherman, perhaps the following will help.

The tree contains the equivalent of six hundred thousand one hundred and twenty board feet of timber, enough to make five thousand million matches. Burning them singly, at a rate of one match every fifteen seconds, means it would take two thousand, three hundred and eighty-one years to burn the tree. Not that the General Sherman will ever be burnt down. Like other *Sequoiadendron giganteum* as they are now called, its disease and fire-resistant bark is over sixty centimetres (two feet) thick.

It's unlikely to be cut down either as together with the rest of the forest, it forms part of the protected Sequoia National Park. The last time one was chopped was in 1875. It took two men nine days to do the job while a third man picked up the chips!

But of all the facts that are known about the General Sherman, there's one nobody is certain of – its age. It's been estimated to be between three thousand and three thousand five hundred years old, but no dendrochronologist, as ring-counters are called,

has yet performed a count, the usual way to determine a tree's age. The reason this hasn't been done is simple. No one has yet made a drill long enough to reach the centre of it!

Possibly the only fact to convey just how big the biggest of all is, is this one:

From the ground to the tree's first large branch is 39.62 metres (130 feet). That branch with a diameter of 2.07 metres (6.8 feet) is bigger and longer than the world's tallest elm.

In the
Tenere Desert
in Africa grows a tree
which is 50 kilometres (31 miles)
from any other. It's the loneliest tree in
the world, but in February 1960 it was
rammed by a French lorry driver.
C'est la vie!

The next time you ride in a car, ask the driver to hold a steady speed of 23.1 miles per hour. Going at that speed means that after twelve hours you would have travelled 446.19 kilometres (277.25 miles). That is exactly what Beryl Burton did on 17 September 1967 – on a bicycle.

Born on 12 May 1937 in Leeds, Beryl started cycling soon after she met her husband-to-be, Charlie, who was a member of the Morley Cycling Club. He lent her a bike so they could ride together on club runs – the start of a hobby that soon led Beryl to racing. Natural ability, hard work, and a determination to improve upon herself has since brought her what is probably the most outstanding list of achievements ever gained by anyone of either sex in any sport.

There are three different types of cycle racing.

Pursuit Racing takes place on a steeply-banked track. Two riders, one on each side of the track, start at the same time and try to catch each other up. If they don't succeed before 3000 metres, the one who has gained most ground at that distance wins.

Road Racing is when all the competitors start at the same time and the first over the finishing line is the winner.

Time Trial is when each competitor sets off at one-minute intervals on the road and rides against the clock. The competitor with the fastest time over a set distance, or the furthest ridden in a set time, is the winner. All time trials are ridden "out and back" so that the riders have to go up all the hills they've ridden down and vice versa.

It is this last type of racing that Beryl prefers, even though she's won the World Ladies' Pursuit Championship *five* times and the World Ladies' Road Race Championship *twice*. She also holds the world record for the 3000-metres standing start (that's nearly two miles), in 4 minutes 14.9 seconds, and the 20 kilometre (12.42 miles) record in 28 minutes 58.4 seconds – that's an average speed of over twenty-five m.p.h.

# BUILT FOR ONE

In National Championships, held annually, Beryl's won the 3000-metres Pursuit *fourteen* times and the Road Race *twelve* times. But it's her favourite event, Time Trials, that she excels in. Since 1958, she's won the twenty-five-mile Time Trial *eighteen* times, the fifty-mile *seventeen* times, and the one-hundred-mile *fifteen* times. Add to that the British Best All-Round Championship – the best average speed set over a season – *sixteen* times.

She's also the national record holder for the following:

| Distance | Hr. | Mins. | Secs. | Date |
| --- | --- | --- | --- | --- |
| 10 miles | | 21 | 25 | 29 April 1973 |
| 25 miles | | 53 | 21 | 17 June 1976 |
| 30 miles | 1 | 12 | 20 | 3 May 1969 |
| 50 miles | 1 | 54 | 7 | 8 July 1973 |
| 100 miles | 3 | 55 | 5 | 4 August 1968 |

In the twelve-hour time trial mentioned at the beginning, Beryl Burton not only captured the record by cycling 277.25 miles in that time, but also beat the man's record – the only woman in the world to have achieved that distinction at a national level in a physical sport.

What makes Beryl so outstanding is impossible to say. Talking to her gives the impression that she's just like thousands of other working Mums in the country. A job on a farm in the daytime (she cycles there and back of course), and running a home for her family the rest of the time, doesn't give any clue that this small, modest Yorkshire lass has the ability to wear out two bicycle frames a year – through metal fatigue!

What makes her a champion on two wheels will forever remain a mystery. What isn't a mystery is the fact that many experts have called her "The world's greatest-ever female athlete".

For her services to the sport, Beryl was awarded the MBE in June 1964 and the OBE in June 1968. To receive them, she travelled to Buckingham Palace – by car!

# TEN GREEN BOTTLES

Ten green bottles hanging on the wall
Ten green bottles hanging on the wall,
And if one quarter-bottle should accidentally fall,
There'd be nine green bottles a-hanging on the wall.

Nine green bottles hanging on the wall
Nine green bottles hanging on the wall,
And if one half-bottle should accidentally fall,
There'd be eight green bottles a-hanging on the wall.

Eight green bottles hanging on the wall
Eight green bottles hanging on the wall,
And if one standard bottle should accidentally fall,
There'd be seven green bottles a-hanging on the wall.

Seven green bottles hanging on the wall
Seven green bottles hanging on the wall,
And if one big magnum should accidentally fall,
There'd be six green bottles a-hanging on the wall.

Six green bottles hanging on the wall
Six green bottles hanging on the wall,
And if one Jeroboam should accidentally fall,
There'd be five green bottles a-hanging on the wall.

Five green bottles hanging on the wall
Five green bottles hanging on the wall,
And if one Rehoboam should accidentally fall,
There'd be four green bottles a-hanging on the wall.

Four green bottles hanging on the wall
Four green bottles hanging on the wall,
And if one Methuselah should accidentally fall,
There'd be three green bottles a-hanging on the wall.

Three green bottles hanging on the wall
Three green bottles hanging on the wall,
And if one Salmanazer should accidentally fall,
There'd be two green bottles a-hanging on the wall.

Two green bottles hanging on the wall
Two green bottles hanging on the wall,
And if one Balthazar should accidentally fall,
There'd be one green bottle a-hanging on the wall.

One green bottle hanging on the wall
One green bottle hanging on the wall,
And if that Nebuchadnezzar should accidentally fall,
There'd be no green bottles a-hanging on the wall . . .

. . . and the only complete set of champagne bottles
known would have been destroyed!

# KNOCK KNOCK—WHO'S THERE?

If your answer to that question is "Smith", congratulations — you're a Record Breaker. Along

you. Between 9.7% and 12.1% of the Chinese population is born with the name "Chang" which

"Hey you" or "Nameless" or even "Oy". According to the forty-seven million names on the Department of Health and Social Security index someone's surname is just that — "Oy". It's one of the four two-letter British surnames in existence, the others being "By", "On" and "Za". There are also five examples of people with a one-lettered surname : "A", "B", "J", "N", and "O".

with about eight hundred thousand more people in Great Britain, you've got the commonest surname in the English-speaking world. But don't shout about it too much because all the "Changs" will certainly drown

means there are at least seventy-five million of them.

Names are something that we've all got in common — it's impossible to live without one. Even if you tried it, other people would give you one, such as

That six-barrelled surname, the longest in the United Kingdom, belonged to a gentleman born in 1884 and who died 20 February 1917. He also had quite a few Christian names — Leone Sextus Denys Oswolf Fraudati filius.

Quite a mouthful, but nothing compared with the daughter of Arthur Pepper of West Derby. Born on 19 December 1882, she was christened with one name for every letter of the alphabet except P — the letter that starts her surname.

KNOCK KNOCK

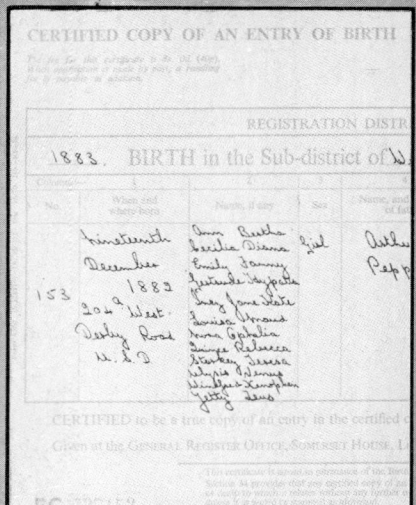

WHO'S THERE?

ANN

ANN
BERTHA
CECILIA
DIANA
EMILY FANNY
GERTRUDE
HYPATIA
INEZ JANE
KATE
LOUISA
MAUD NORA
OPHELIA
QUINCE
REBECCA
STARKEY
TERESA
ULYSIS VENUS
WINIFRED
XENOPHEN
YETTY
ZEUS
PEPPER

ANN WHO?

Like A B C D E F G H I J K L M N O Q R S T U V W X Y Z Pepper, most of us put up with the names given to us by our parents at birth.

Some people however change their name in order to "make a name for themselves".

Julia Elizabeth Wells became Julie Andrews.

Harry Webb became Cliff Richard.

Arnold Dorsey became Englebert Humperdinck.

Norma Jean Baker became Marilyn Monroe.

Les Hope became Bob Hope, presumably because he didn't like being nicknamed "Hope-less".

Name changes occur for all sorts of reasons. Zeke Zzzypt took his name so as to be last in the local telephone directory in San Francisco, California. He was recently pushed up a place by Zachary Zzzzra. In Miami, Florida, Vladimir Zzzyd did the same thing to Zero Zzzzz. In Los Angeles however, a private company surpassed them all.

ADOLPH
BLAINE
CHARLES
DAVID
EARL
FREDERICK
GERALD
HUBERT
IRVIN
JOHN
KENNETH
LLOYD
MARTIN
NERO
OLIVER
PAUL
QUINCY
RANDOLPH
SHERMAN
THOMAS
UNCAS
VICTOR
WILLIAM
XERXES
YANCY
ZEUS

"A name for every letter in the alphabet — how did you manage to get them all?"

"When I was born, my family put a whole alphabetical list of names in a container and were going to pick out one or two. But instead of that they gave me the lot."

"And which of them do you use?"

"I use Hubert because it means brilliant mind — and you have to have a brilliant mind not only to remember all my Christian names but my surname as well".

"I don't think Zeus is a difficult name to remember?"

"Zeus isn't my surname you know, it's my twenty-sixth Christian name. My surname is

"How many letters has it got ?"

"591"

"What does it mean ?"

"Well it's Germanic in origin and roughly translated it means : a wolf-killer who lives in a stone house in a shepherd's village where the sheep are well fed and guarded from voracious enemies, whose ancestors one million two hundred thousand years before the first earth man decided to come to a star which had a habitable planet on which to establish a new race, which would be free from war and strife, and also from attack from any race of inter-solar space."

"Now has that always been your name, or did you change it ?"

"That is the genuine family name, but I've shortened it to Wolfstern for everyday purposes mainly because when I have to fill in a form that says "give your full name", there's not room for all of mine !"

Roy Castle "Nameograph" — a self-portrait using the nine letters of his name. When you've found them try making one out of your own name.

# LIGHTNING ROD

The odds against anyone being struck by lightning are millions to one. The odds against them living to tell of the experience are even greater. But there's one man in the world who's beaten all the odds because he's been struck by lightning no less than five times. He's Roy Sullivan, who for thirty-four years has been a Ranger in the Shenandoah National Park in the Blue Ridge Mountains of Virginia. In 1974 Roy, known to his friends as "Lightning Rod", told us how he was always "in the wrong place at the wrong time".

"Well the first time the elements got me was in April 1942. There was a terrible storm, and I was just passing under a telephone line on my way towards the Millers Head Fire Tower when the lightning came down and hit the wire. It travelled along the wire and then when it got to me, it jumped off and struck me on the head. It burnt a strip down my leg about half an inch wide, made a hole in my shoe and knocked my big toe-nail off.

"I was a bit shaken, I don't mind telling you, and the amazing thing about that hit was that I was carrying a watch in my pocket and the lightning went right through one side of it and out the other – stopped it for good – at 3.30, the time of the strike."

And what about the second time you were struck?

"That was a good many years later – in 1969. I was driving a Government vehicle on the Skyline Drive during a pretty fierce thunderstorm, and just when I got to Chalmers Gap at my Outpost 97, a bolt struck two trees on the right side of the truck. I saw them both come down. Then it came right through the truck, catching me on the side of the head. Burnt my eyebrows, eyelashes and all the hair up to my hat brim. Then it went on through and struck another tree, killing all three trees. I was knocked unconscious, and the truck finally came to a stop half-way up a steep bank. I came to eventually – but I remember that for some minutes I couldn't see or hear anything."

You must have thought that it couldn't happen again.

"I sure did, but in the following year, 1970, there was a storm in Waynesboro, just four miles from where we live in Sawmill Run. I just walked outside the house to see if any of the rain was coming our way, because we hadn't had any for some time and the garden was getting a little dry. I'd just got down to the end of the garden when this streak of lightning comes out of a small cloud . . . of course you can't dodge it . . . and that caught me on the left shoulder, went down my left arm and the left leg, and turned me for a loop in the air. I landed about ten feet away with second degree burns down the whole left side of my body."

So you were struck two years running? What about the following year?

"I had a real good year in 1971 – I dodged every storm! Then one day, in April '72, I was working at the Loft Mountain Restoration Station when it pulled a real sneaky one on me. Caught me on the back of the head while I wasn't looking and set my hair on fire. I rushed to a wash basin but couldn't get my head in. Either the basin was too small or my head was too large. Anyway, I managed to extinguish the fire in the end, but I finished up with some pretty nasty blisters.

"I should have been more prepared for that one because in March I'd

*Hot News! On 5 June 1976 Roy Sullivan was struck by lightning for a sixth time. His only injury was a burnt ankle!*

had a dream that I was going to be struck in April, and I've had too many dreams come true not to believe them.

"Then in June 1973 I had a dream that I was going to get strike number five in July. Well, I just went out of my way to avoid every storm that month and I was lucky enough to succeed. But my luck didn't hold for long, because in August there was one very bad storm which I could see was working in from the south to where I was parked at the Loft Mountain Wayside Restaurant. I said to myself, 'This is no place for Roy' and started to drive north to get out of its way. I'd gone about ten miles when I thought I'd stop to see whether the storm was travelling faster or slower than I was. Well, the storm was still a fair distance away, but just above me was this one little cloud, and out of it came the fifth bolt of lightning. It caught me plum on the head, burnt a hole in my hat and set my hair on fire again. Then it went down my body and set my underclothes on fire as well. Luckily I had a five-gallon can of water in the truck which I poured all over me, but boy, I sure was hot for a few minutes."

Have you had any more dreams ?

"I certainly have. Shortly after strike number five I dreamt that I was never going to be hit by lightning again — and so far that dream's true."

Why do you think this keeps happening to you ?

"I don't know, it hasn't happened to any other Ranger in the Park. Maybe God is trying to prove something. There's a saying that 'lightning never strikes in the same place twice'. As far as my experiences are concerned that's true. Every time it happened to me I was in a different place. Fate, I suppose, just put me in the wrong place at the wrong time."

Even though Roy Sullivan, the only man living to be struck by lightning five times, cannot disprove the saying "lightning never strikes in the same place twice", these photographs can. They show the Empire State building in New York City, for thirty-nine years the tallest building in the world, on three of the many occasions it's been hit by lightning.

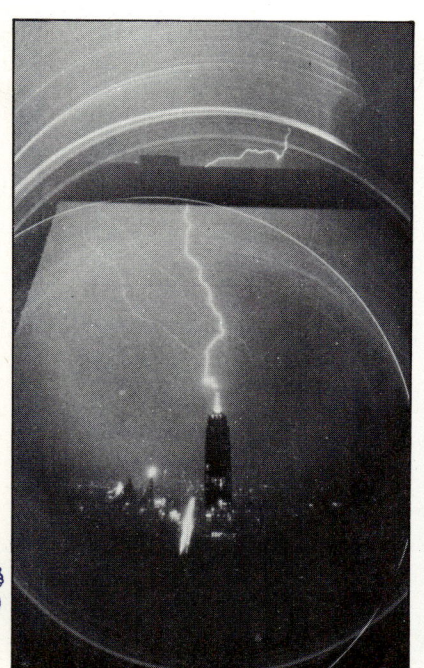

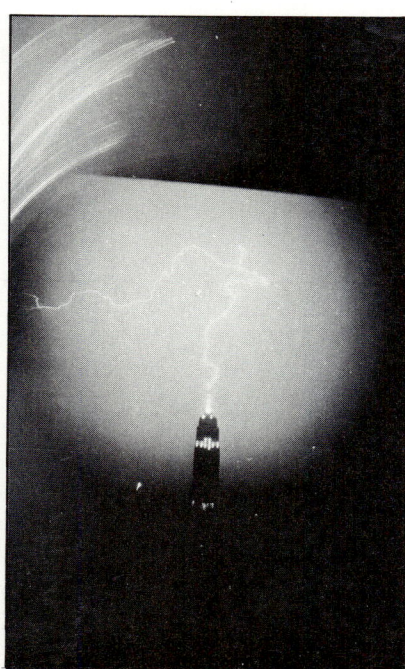

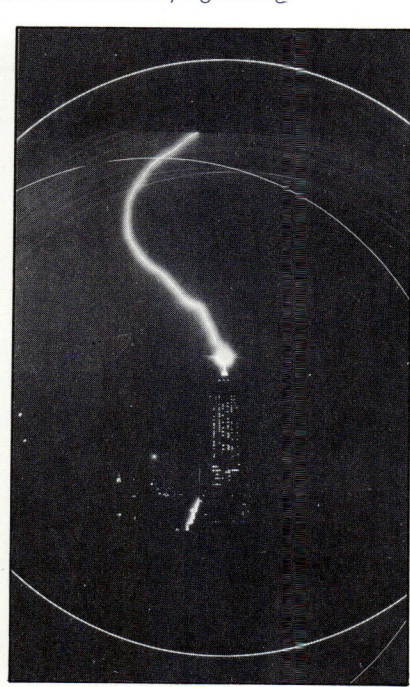

# A CRICK IN THE NECK-

— that's what you get after an afternoon talking to Christopher Paul Greener — unless you ask him to sit down. And the reason is he's tall, he's extremely tall, in fact he's Britain's tallest fully mobile man and barefooted is 226.6 cm (7ft 5¼ins) tall.

Chris, who now lives in Hayes, Kent, was born in New Brighton, Merseyside, on 21 November 1943, since when he's grown, and grown, and grown. As a schoolboy he was taller than most of his teachers and at an age when most people stop growing, he just carried on. But he's stopped now — he thinks.

Being very tall means he's able to see easily at soccer matches and things like that, and he doesn't need a step ladder to paint the ceiling, but there are many disadvantages too, and Chris's main one is clothes. Everything has to be specially made — suits and shirts, trousers and ties, socks and shoes (size 16, would you believe?).

Travel, too, has its problems. On the London Underground one day, in a forgetful moment, he suddenly stood up, smashed a bulb with his head and put all the lights out. Buses are smaller — "almost impossible" he says — unlike trains which are fine for Chris, but not very pleasant for the person sitting opposite. How would you like to spend a journey staring into a pair of somebody else's knees?

Luckily Chris doesn't have to worry about public transport very much as he's got his own car. He has to practically sit in the back seat to drive it — but drive it he does. He cycles too — on what is probably the world's biggest bike.

Seeing he's so tall you would think he comes from a very tall

23

Robert Wadlow  272cms  8' 11.1''
Chris Greener  227cms  7' 5¼''
Norris McWhirter  175cms  5' 9''
Roy Castle  169cms  5' 6½''

family, but that isn't true. His father's 190.5cm (6ft 3ins) and his Mum's 167.6 cm (5ft 6ins). Chris calls her "Titch" – and she must often suffer, like I did after an afternoon with Chris, from a crick in the neck !

Even at 226.6 cm (7ft 5¼ins) Chris isn't the tallest man that the world has ever known. Three thousand years ago Goliath of Gath was supposedly six cubits and a span (290 cm (9ft 6½ins)), but no one can prove it, and many circus giants claim heights of over 275 cm (9ft 0⅝in), but won't let themselves be impartially measured.

In the last hundred years, on evidence collected by the medical profession, the tallest man ever was Robert Pershing Wadlow. He was born at 6.30 am on 22 February 1918 in Alton, Illinois, USA, and weighed 3 kg 860 (8½ lbs). He grew as follows :

Robert Wadlow celebrating his twenty-first birthday with his family

| Age in years | Height | |
|---:|---|---|
| 5 | 163 cm | 5'4'' |
| 8 | 183 cm | 6'0'' |
| 9 | 189 cm | 6'2½'' |
| 10 | 196 cm | 6'5'' |
| 11 | 200 cm | 6'7'' |
| 12 | 210 cm | 6'10½'' |
| 13 | 218 cm | 7'1¾'' |
| 14 | 226 cm | 7'5'' |
| 15 | 234 cm | 7'8'' |
| 16 | 240 cm | 7'10½'' |
| 17 | 245 cm | 8'0½'' |
| 18 | 253 cm | 8'3½'' |
| 19 | 258 cm | 8'5½'' |
| 20 | 261 cm | 8'6¾'' |
| 21 | 265 cm | 8'8¼'' |

Robert Wadlow died of a foot disease at 1.30 am on 15 July 1940 in Manistee, Michigan, just eighteen days after being measured by Dr C. M. Charles, Associate Professor of Anatomy at Washington University's School of Medicine in St Louis, Missouri. His height then was an incredible 272 cm (8ft 11.1 ins).

# WATER MUSIC

Roy Castle tells of a very unusual invitation he received in Bermuda

*You are invited to a*
*Grand Concert*
*at the*
*Swimming Pool*
*to hear a performance of*
*Vivaldi's Violin Concerto*
*played by*
*Mark Gottlieb*
*on the world's first Aqualin*

❝I couldn't resist the temptation as I'd never heard of an aqualin before and, dressed for the occasion, duly arrived at the swimming pool. The strains of Vivaldi's Violin Concerto were already ringing around the pool, but the soloist, Mark Gottlieb, was nowhere to be seen.

Then someone pointed to a dark shape in the middle of the pool. If Mark was taking the trouble to give the performance underwater, the least I could do was to listen to it in the same place – so in I went.
Looking around, it appeared that I was the only member of the audience underwater, so when the performance was finished I took the opportunity to ask 18-year-old Mark how it all began.

The son of a music professor at the Evergreen State College, Olympia, USA, he first started playing the violin at the age of seven, but was always more interested in swimming and diving than in music. Studying to be an oceanographer, Mark wanted to experiment with the effects of sounds under water and decided an underwater violin – an aqualin – might help him. So he went about making one.

A cheap violin, marine varnished twice, was his first effort and, on trying it, Mark came up against his first snag. The strings, which had been tuned correctly above water, changed pitch when taken below and the wooden tuning pegs, having expanded when wet, could not be moved. He overcame this by using metal tuning pegs instead of wooden ones.

With that problem resolved he tried again, only to realise that because water is so much denser than air, no one but himself could hear the aqualin. His answer was an electric guitar microphone – waterproofed of course – attached to the violin with a cable feeding an amplifier on dry land. The amplifier fed two loudspeakers – one on land and one underwater. That way anyone who wanted to could hear the performance above as well as below the water – aqua-stereo !

The aqualin was successful, so I asked him about the possibility of an underwater orchestra. Mark replied that he was already working on an underwater organ – a hydrorgan he called it – and that when it was finished he and his sister would be giving some duets. Until then, he would have to stick to solos – unless, of course, I wanted to join him on my trumpet.

I was only too keen to have a try, and we performed what can only be described as the most authentic "performance" of Handel's Water Music that has ever been played. There was only one snag – no one was underwater to hear it.

# SIOUXEEE!

In February 1973, at the Grand Hotel, Scarborough, Margaret Featherstone shouted "Siouxeee" at the top of her voice. Two metres away was a microphone connected to a sound measuring device, and Margaret's voice registered one hundred and six decibels on the machine. This meant that Margaret had become the winner of the first Women's World Shouting Championship. All the competitors in the contest were allowed three shouts, but they could only shout "Siouxeee", a word devised because it allows the optimum range in many languages – an international word!

Decibel is the name of the unit used to measure the intensity, or loudness, of sound. Normal conversation between two people standing about a metre apart would register between sixty and eighty decibels, so although Margaret's shout of one hundred and six decibels might not seem much higher, in fact it is when you learn that intensity is measured on a logarithmic scale.

To try and explain what that means, one must start with the quietest sound anyone can hear – the "threshold of hearing". Almost total silence, with an intensity of one is the same as zero decibels. The rustle of a few leaves in the breeze will register about ten decibels, an intensity increase of ten. A very quiet whisper would be about twenty decibels – an intensity increase of one hundred. The tick of a watch about thirty decibels – an intensity of one thousand. In other words, for every ten decibels *added*, the intensity is *multiplied* by ten.

What this means is that Margaret's shout of one hundred and six decibels is over ten thousand million times more intense than the least audible sound, or one thousand times more intense than normal conversation.

Margaret Featherstone

Joan Whitehead

Not content with a hundred and six decibels, Margaret Featherstone went to the Spa Grand Hall in 1974 to defend her world title – and the best of her three "Siouxeee's" was recorded at a hundred and nine point seven decibels – a new world shouting record.

Undefeated for two years, Margaret decided to retire so when the 1975 Championship came along, the title went to Joan Whitehead, landlady of "The Spotted Cow Inn", York. A new shouting champion but, with only a hundred and five decibels, not a new record.

In 1976 Joan Whitehead has taken the title again with a hundred and eight decibels – still not a new record, but getting closer and closer. Perhaps in 1977 Margaret will come out of retirement to challenge Joan – and perhaps the record will go a bit higher. If it does, let's hope it doesn't reach a hundred and twenty decibels, which is considered to be for the listener, the "threshold of pain". It would be like standing on a runway listening to a jet aircraft taking off under full power – that's some "Siouxeee"!

# THE FIRST FOUR-MINUTE MILE

The year  1954
The date  6 May
The time  18.10
The place  Iffley Road
   Athletic Track, Oxford
The Meeting  Oxford University
   v. Amateur Athletic Association
The official announcer
   Norris McWhirter

The victorious Roger Bannister with Chris Brasher (left) and Chris Chataway (right) shortly after his historic first sub-four-minute-mile

"Ladies and gentlemen, here is the result of event number nine, the One Mile : First, number 41, R. G. Bannister, of the Amateur Athletic Association and formerly of Exeter and Merton Colleges, with a time which is a new meeting and track record and which, subject to ratification, will be a new English Native, British (National), British (All-Comers'), European, British Empire and World's Record. The time is three . . ."

The rest of that announcement was never heard. The crowd erupted when they heard the word "three", because to them that could mean only one thing — the greatest dream of the athletic world had been achieved — the phantom four-minute mile had finally been beaten — in 3 minutes 59.4 seconds.

   For years Australian John Landy, American Wes Santee, and all the other leading milers in the world had been battering away at the

4 minute 1.3 seconds set by Sweden's Gunther Hagg in 1945. And all of them were not only trying to break that record — but were taking part in another race — a world-wide race — to be the first sub-four-minute-miler.

Norris McWhirter, life-long friend of Roger Bannister and himself an Oxford sprinter, takes up the inside story in which he was personally involved.

Four-minute-mile fever had been around for some time, and nobody was more conscious of its increase in temperature than Bannister himself. So, as the Oxford University v. AAA fixture was the first major competition of our summer season, 6 May became the day.

Roger had long before enlisted the help of his two friends and training colleagues Chris Chataway of Oxford and Olympic Steeplechaser Chris Brasher of Cambridge, and they had been planning the assault since the previous November. During the winter, I attended a great number of training sessions in which I was literally the only witness. They were often done in bleak conditions on a filthy black cinder track in Paddington. There I used to time Roger's fiendish repetition of interval training. This is necessary to inure the body to the punishment and get it resistant to the lack of oxygen, which is involved in running any longish distance at an unnaturally fast pace.

This was his immediate preparation :
12 April  7 × 880 yards in 33 minutes
14 April  ¾ mile solo in 3 :02.0 (laps 61, 61 and 60 secs.)
15 April  880 yards solo in 1 :53.0
16-19 April  Rock climbing in Scotland
22 April  10 × 440 yards (1st lap 56.3 – last lap 56.3 – average 58.9)
24 April  ¾ mile with Chataway in 3 :00.0
26 April  ¾ mile in 3 :14.0 ; 8 minutes rest ; ¾ mile in 3 :08.6
28 April  ¾ mile solo in 2 :59.0 in high wind
30 April  880 yards in 1 :54.0
1-5 May  Rest

On the morning of Thursday, 6 May, while I was having the track surveyed to check the distance (it was, in fact, two inches over the mile), Roger Bannister travelled to Oxford from London by train with Franz Stampfl, his adviser. They talked of nothing except the strong wind that was whistling through the swaying trees. It was this howling wind that was to be the deciding factor as to whether or not the attempt would be made later in the day.

After a lunch of ham salad and prunes at the home of his friends Charles and Eileen Wenden, and the afternoon spent playing with their children, Roger arrived at the track at 5 pm — an hour before the race. He was very despondent about the wind. Franz Stampfl insisted that no decision should be made about attempting the four-minute mile before the three conspirators had warmed up. Fifteen minutes before the start he asked the trio if it was on, first to Chris Brasher. Answer – "Yes". Then to Chris Chataway – "Neutral". Lastly to Bannister – "No".

With five minutes to go, Stampfl tried again, this time pointing out that the wind had suddenly slackened. Brasher – "Yes". Chataway – "Yes". Bannister – "No". But after a final hundred and fifty yards fast stride, and seeing that the wind had obviously dropped, Bannister put on his spikes and said "Yes". It was on.

Six men lined up for the start. Bannister, Brasher, Chataway, Bill Hulatt, the American George Dole and Alan Gordon.

Chris Chataway takes the bell ahead of Roger Bannister at the start of the fourth and final lap

The timekeepers press their stopwatches as Roger crosses the finishing line. Norris McWhirter, in white sweater, is on the right holding the microphone

After a false start (Brasher was too keen to get going), the race was under way and the plan for the attempt was put into practice. Brasher went straight into the lead, with Bannister second and Chataway third. The plan was that Brasher should run the first two laps in under two minutes and carry on in the lead at the same pace for as long as possible. Then on the command "Chris" from Bannister, Chataway was to take over the lead until Bannister "headed for home" with 220 yards to go.

It worked almost perfectly. After the first half a furlong Bannister yelled "faster" to Brasher because he thought he was going too slow. Brasher ignored him and was proved to be right – they went through the half mile in 1:58.0. After two and a half laps, the command came and Chataway took over. The bell was tolled at 3:00.4. With 230 yards left, Bannister pulled out to start that heart-rending drive for the sanctuary of the tape. My brother Ross, the only 1,500 metres time-keeper, saw him flash by in 3:43.0 – equal to the world record for that distance.

With his pulse at a hundred and fifty-five, his face strained and white, and all colour vision drained from his eyes, Bannister flashed over the line in 3 minutes 59.4 seconds. He'd done it – the world's first sub-four-minute mile.

On 29 April, a week before the event took place, the staff of *Athletics World*, of which Norris McWhirter was co-editor with his late brother Ross, made their forecasts of Bannister's time. They were as follows : Patricia Troop 4:01.8   Neil Allen 4:01.2   Norris McWhirter 3:59.5

# READ ALL ABOUT IT!

HOC EST
NOVUM TESTAMENTUM
ÆGYPTIUM vulgo COPTICUM
Ex MSS. BODLEJANIS descripsit,
Cum Vaticanis et Parisiensibus contulit,
et in Latinum sermonem convertit
DAVID WILKINS
Ecclesiæ Anglicanæ Presbyter.
OXONII,
E Theatro Sheldoniano Typis et Sumptibus Academiæ, 1716.

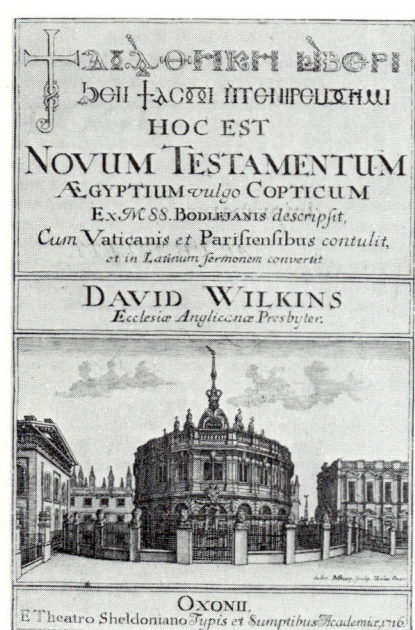

The title page of the Coptic New Testament

This book is a book of records – a record book – a book of record breakers. What it isn't is a record-breaking book – a book-breaking record or a record book of records.

It is, in fact, just one of over twenty thousand new titles that are published in Britain every year, some of which, though not about records, are record breakers in themselves.

In 1716, five hundred copies of the New Testament, translated by David Wilkins from Latin into the remote language of Coptic were published by the Oxford University Press. But only one book was sold, on average, every one hundred and thirty-nine days, so the five hundred original copies lasted for one hundred and ninety-one years. Even though it's the world's slowest seller, the Bible in Coptic was reprinted in 1969, and if anyone has trouble finding it, they should try Blackwell's in Oxford, the world's largest academic book shop. With a staff of seven hundred and fifty, over twenty thousand suppliers and one hundred and ten thousand customers in one hundred and thirty-three countries, they claim to be able to get practically any book that's ever been published anywhere in the world, and if *that* isn't a claim to fame, the Norrington room in the shop certainly has one. With a floor area of over nine hundred and twenty-nine square metres, and more than four kilometres of shelving, containing one hundred and sixty thousand volumes, it holds the record for being the largest display of books in one room in the world.

The Norrington Room

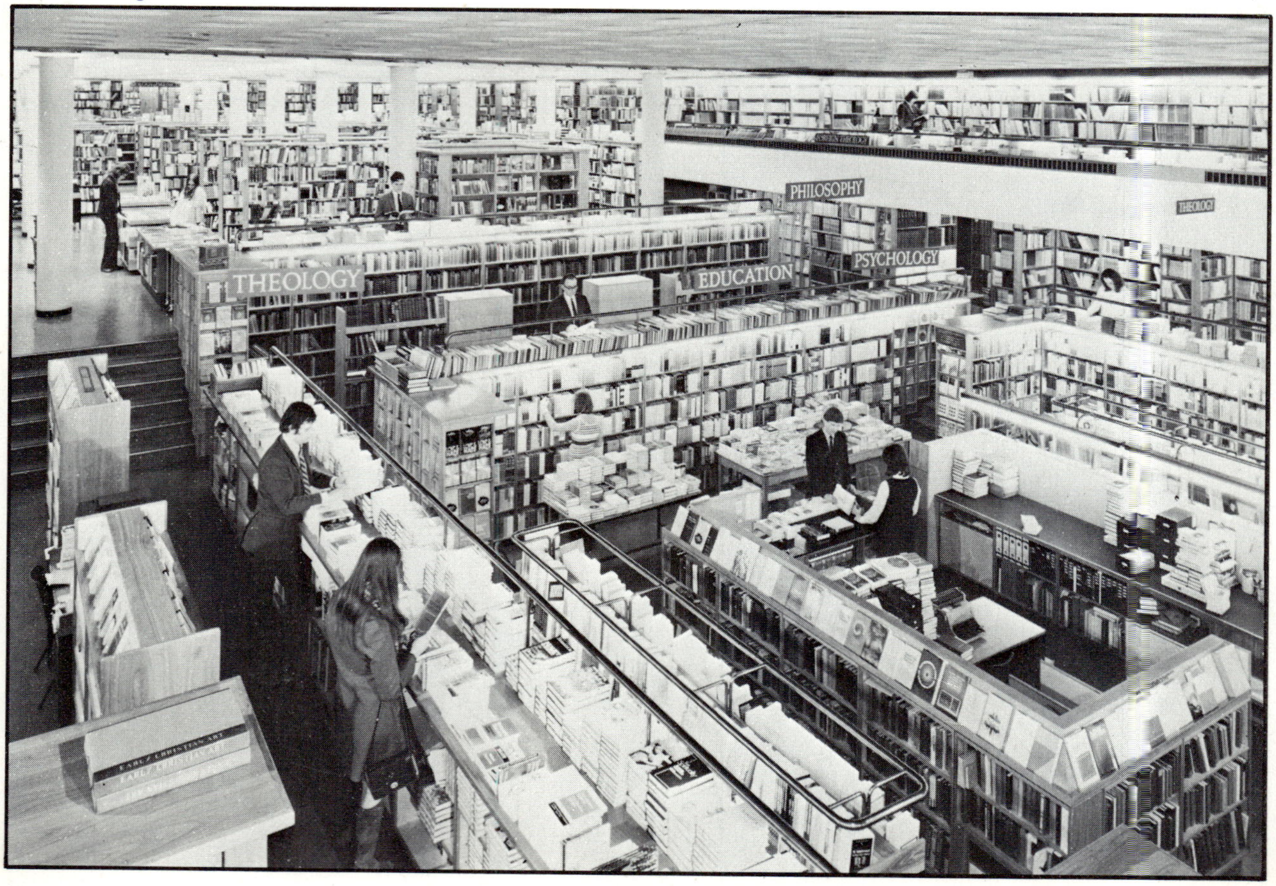

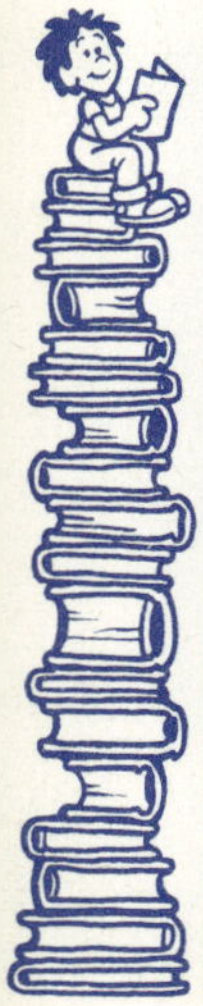

A book you'll certainly find there is one written by Sir Harold Hartley, record holder for being the world's slowest author. On 22 February 1901, he made an agreement with the Oxford University Press to publish *History of Chemistry*, which finally appeared in April 1971, over seventy years later.

Roy Castle studying *The History of Chemistry*

The actual size of the world's smallest book. Magnified are pages 24 and 25

There's one book that's difficult to find anywhere. It's the smallest book printed from metal type in the world. 2.9 mm square and 1.5 mm thick, it was printed in a limited edition of twenty-five at Gleniffer Press, Paisley, Scotland, in 1975. It contains the alphabet, one letter per page, and presumably was easy enough to write. Some people say, of course, that writing is only words. The snag is that in the twelve-volume Royal quarto Oxford English Dictionary, the largest in the world, there are four hundred and fourteen thousand, eight hundred and twenty-five of them listed – and that's not including the two supplements !

A lot of words were used in *Les Miserables*, which in classical western literature has the longest sentence. It contains eight hundred and twenty words, punctuated by ninety-three comas, fifty-one semi-colons ; four dashes – and one full stop. Victor Hugo, its author, also holds another record. He was away on holiday when his book was published but, anxious to know how it was selling, he decided to send his publishers a letter. He wrote :

His publisher, Hurst and Blackett, knowing what the question was, replied in the same style. They wrote :

— thus establishing a record for the shortest ever correspondence — all because of a book !

There are a great many records about books but there's only one "record book of records". That belongs to the world's all-time best seller, the *Guinness Book of Records*. First published in October 1955, total sales in fourteen languages surpassed the twenty-three million, nine hundred and sixteen thousand of Dr Benjamin Spock's *The Common Sense Book of Baby and Child Care* in November 1974.

See page 48 for what is probably the world's most boring book

# DID YOU KNOW...

. . . that it took only 10.9 seconds for thirteen-year-old Kenneth L. Purnell of Calgary, Alberta, Canada, to tie a square knot, sheet bend, sheep shank, clove hitch, round turn and two half hitches and bowline (the six *Scout Handbook* knots) on individual ropes on 23 February 1974 !

. . . that Connie Baker of Los Angeles, USA, in April 1975, swung fifty-eight hula hoops simultaneously round her torso from a dead start !

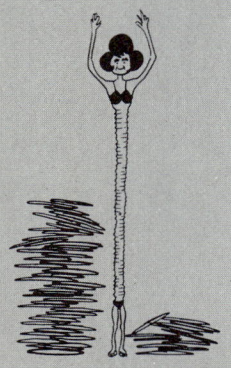

# OODLES OF NOODLES

There's pea soup and soup
　　made with onions
There's ox-tail and pig-tail as well –
But this soup is super it's just
　　like a dream
And oh, what a luverly smell.

There's Oodles of Noodles,
Yes ! Noodles in Oodles,
In my chicken soup !

The flavour's a winner,
And when it's for dinner,
The kids give a whoop !

Dad thinks it grand,
And he eats it with zest,
While Granny, who knows
Says, "It beats all the rest"
Now ! Who'll have a plateful
To prove it's the best !

For, there's Oodles of Noodles,
Yes ! Noodles in Oodles,
Just Oodles of Noodles
In my chicken soup.

Those words are from an old
 song written by Denis Breeze and
Conrad Leonard. But you don't
have "Oodles of Noodles" only in
chicken soup –

– you'll find them in a wide variety of dishes all over the world.

Originally from China, where they were an alternative to pancakes and bread, they found their way into many Indian and Arab dishes in the early thirteenth century.

In 1299, the famous explorer Marco Polo returned to Venice with some Chinese noodles, which the Italians quickly found how to make, and which today are included in many famous Italian recipes.

Noodles are one of many different types of pasta, a dough-like substance that is made into different shapes. Other types include mezzani, spaghetti, spaghettini, fedelini and the very thin capellini. All these are straight varieties of spaghetti but of varying thicknesses. Then there are the fancy-shaped ones – corkscrew tortiglioni, butterfly farfalle and wheel-shaped ruote. Add to those nocchette, semini, acini di pepe and conchigliette, don't forget macaroni and cannelloni, and you've got an idea just how useful pasta is in cooking.

How do you make it ? And more important, how do you make it into thread-like noodles ? Stephen Yim, a Chinese chef in a famous restaurant in London, gave us his simple recipe : Flour, a pinch of salt, an egg, cooking oil, water, and a splash of soda water. Mix them together to a smooth paste. and you're ready to make the solid piece of dough into noodles.

To give an idea how it's done, Stephen gave a demonstration of a skill that's normally only seen by the staff on the other side of the kitchen door. After rolling out the dough to make one thick noodle, he then proceeded to stretch, throw, twist and turn it until it was long enough to fold into two. Using a technique that can only be described as incredible, he continued stretching, throwing, hitting, pulling and twisting, folding the two noodles into four thinner ones, the four into eight, eight into sixteen, sixteen into thirty-two, thirty-two into sixty-four, sixty-four into one hundred and twenty-eight and one hundred and twenty-eight into two hundred and fifty-six.

Each of the noodles, or mien as they're known in Chinese, was over 1.52 metres (five feet) long and to make all two hundred and fifty-six had taken him only sixty-three seconds.

Stephen Yim came to *The Record Breakers* with a reputation of being the fastest noodle maker in the world. He left having proved it.

# ANYONE CARE FOR A WALK?

According to the International Amateur Athletic Federation walking is "progression by steps so taken that unbroken contact with the ground is maintained." The definition also states that "the leg must be straightened (ie not bent at the knee) at least for one moment."

For someone competing in an official walking race those rules must be strictly adhered to, otherwise disqualification will follow. But most people who walk do it without thinking. Walking to school or taking a leisurely stroll through the woods is not going to disqualify anyone from anything, and doesn't take much effort. Because normal walking is relatively easy, it's not surprising to find that most people who've got their names in the record books have walked either a very long way or for a very long time – or both.

David Kunst started walking from Waseca, Minnesota, on 10 June 1970. He arrived home on 5 October 1974 having walked 27,360 kilometres (17,000 miles) and was the first person recorded to have "walked round the world".

Not all walking record breakers have achieved that distance however – Plennie L. Wingo of Abeline, Texas, only covered 12,875 kilometres (8,000 miles) from 15 April 1931 to 24 October 1932 on his walk from Santa Monica, California, to Istanbul in Turkey. But he did it walking backwards, and it's regarded as the greatest feat of reverse pedestrianism that the world's ever seen.

If that record sounds too difficult to beat, why not try a shorter one? If you can walk 1,400 kilometres (871 miles) in under fifty-five days, averaging more than 2.54 kilometres per hour (1.58 miles per hour), you'll beat the record set up by Johann Hurlinger of Austria in 1900. At first glance it might seem easy, until you read the rules – you have to cover the distance the same way Johann did – walking on your hands!

Still too difficult? Then have a go at the one Henri Rochetain of France holds. He took three hours twenty minutes to walk only 3,465

David Kunst

Plennie L. Wingo

metres (3,790 yards) on 13 July 1969. Now that is easy – but not the way he did it – on a tightrope slung across a gorge at Clermont Ferrand, France.

As well as holding the record for the longest high wire walk, Henri Rochetain also holds the tightrope endurance record. On 28 March 1973, he stepped onto a wire 120 metres (394 feet) long, 25 metres (82 feet) above a supermarket in Saint Etienne.

He ate, drank and, to the amazement of doctors, slept on the wire until 29 September – one hundred and eighty-five days later. During that time it's estimated he walked over 500 kilometres (three hundred and ten miles) on the wire to keep fit.

Henri Rochetain's records should only be attempted by experts as they are extremely dangerous. Like most walkers it's best to keep your feet on the ground and that's just what John Lees did in 1972.

On 11 April he set off from City Hall, Los Angeles, California. On 3 June he arrived at City Hall, New York City, having walked the 4,628 kilometres (2,875 miles) across the United States. Averaging 86.495 kilometres (53.746 miles) a day, John completed the walk in fifty-three days, twelve hours and fifteen minutes, which at that time was faster than anyone had run across it !

John first started walking to combat asthma – he'd been a chronic sufferer for years – and by walking to work, walking at lunchtimes, walking home, walking in the evenings and walking at weekends, he was soon fit enough to walk from Land's End to John O'Groats.

With that completed, he decided to attempt the North America Coast to Coast, a walk which took him through thirteen States. At times he encountered temperatures that reached 43.3°C (110°F) and fell to almost freezing in the same day. For most of the journey he wore the same pair of shoes – they had to be repaired four times !

Like all walkers who race, John is able to reach a speed of over 12.874 kilometres (8.00 miles) an hour by using the hip pivoting method that gives an increased stride length. Although walkers may look comical to the layman when they're racing, it does mean they are able to keep, even if it is only for a moment, at least one foot on the ground.

Henri Rochetain                    John Lees

# SMILE PLEASE

This photograph was taken on *The Record Breakers* on 3 December 1974.

The camera used was a Japanese "Petal", owned and lent to us by Mr Ted Rosenberg who lives in New Jersey in the United States.

The "Petal", so called because of its circular shape, is 2.9 cm in diameter and 1.65 cm thick. It has a focal length of 12 mm, a shutter speed of 1/25 of a second, and a time exposure. Apart from cameras used for heart surgery and espionage, it's the smallest camera that's ever been sold.

The circular negative – this is the actual size – takes 6 circular  pictures (one of them didn't come out!), each one just 5 mm in diameter. Your turn Norris, smile please.

# ON TOP OF THE WORLD

Wally Herbert, the leader of the British Trans-Arctic Expedition

At the top of the world, bordered by Greenland, North America, Alaska and the USSR, is the Arctic Ocean. What makes it different from all the other oceans on earth is that most of the surface, for most of the year, is ice.

On 21 February 1968, four men with sledges set off from Point Barrow, Alaska, in an attempt to cross the Arctic Ocean and land at the Seven Island Archipelago, north-east of Spitsbergen, 3,090 kilometres (1,920 miles) away.

If they succeeded, theirs would be the longest sustained journey in the history of polar exploration, and one of the last great challenges left to man on Earth would have been overcome.

The four men who made up the British Trans-Arctic Expedition, as it was called, were Dr Roy "Fritz" Koerner, a glaciologist, Allan Gill, a geophysicist, Major Ken Hedges, a doctor in the Royal Army Medical Corps, and Wally Herbert, the leader of the Expedition and the man whose idea it was to make "the longest, loneliest walk in the world" across a "horizontal Everest".

Their departure was the culmination of four years' meticulous planning and the start of a journey that was to last four hundred and sixty-four days in temperatures that never rose above 3°C (37.4°F) and sometimes fell to —47°C (—52.6°F).

As the frozen Arctic Ocean is never still — the ice is drifting all the time — and because of leads or giant gaps which open in the ice so that detours are constantly having to be made, Wally Herbert calculated that they would need to travel nearly double the distance shown on the map to achieve their objective.

To complete the journey in sixteen months, during which it would be possible to travel in only eight, the team would have to average 20.9 statute route kilometres (13 miles) per day, an average that could not be maintained carrying heavy loads.

To overcome this the team would need supplies to be air-dropped at certain points during the journey. The exact positions and times were to be relayed to the fifth member of the team, radio operator Squadron-Leader Freddie Church. Throughout the whole trip he would be the expedition's link with the outside world, being based first at Point Barrow, then moving to the American Scientific Drifting Camp T-3 on the Arctic Ocean, and finally to Spitsbergen for the last stage of the journey — the object being that he would never be more than 805 kilometres (500 miles) from the main party.

The earliest date on which the expedition could leave Point Barrow was 1 February, the latest, 21 February. Only during those three weeks of the year was there a chance that new ice would be packed tightly enough between the coast and the polar ice pack to enable a crossing to be made — a dash across a belt of mush-ice 128 kilometres (80 miles) wide.

For three weeks the team waited impatiently for the right weather conditions then, with the temperature at —40°C (—40°F), the four men took their first steps on the Arctic Ocean. Everyone had his own self-contained sledge, pulled by ten Greenland huskies. Wally Herbert had chosen this individual method of travel so that they need meet only if they ran into some obstacle, or when they camped at the end

Allan Gill navigates his sledge over a pressure ice ridge a few miles north of Barrow

of the day. In that way each man had the companionship of the others to look forward to. For convenience they slept two men to a tent but changed partners every twenty-eight days to avoid the "two tent split" which frequently occurs on long polar expeditions and which results in the two partnerships becoming almost strangers to each other.

During the first few weeks of the journey the team was in constant danger, scrambling over moving ice that was in darkness for twelve hours every day.

By 10 May, having sledged 1,448 route kilometres (900 miles) across vast areas of ice barely thick enough to support the weight of a sledge, summer was rapidly approaching. Because of melting ice, they were forced to convert their sledges into boats to ferry dogs and equipment

across the many leads that by this time were opening up. Averaging only 3.2 kilometres (2 miles) a day, and way behind schedule, they struggled on in a north-west heading, but a drifting maze of shattered ice floes carried them 128 kilometres (80 miles) off course to the east. The last seven days before setting up summer camp on 4 July were to be the worst of their entire journey.

During July and August, living in "Meltville" — two tents and a marquee constructed out of parachutes that had dropped their supplies — the team spent the summer doing scientific studies and drifting 277.8 kilometres (172.6 miles) due north. Even so, they were still far behind the scheduled plan.

On a treacherous surface of thin ice and knee-deep channels of slush,

An aerial picture of Wally Herbert, "Fritz" Koerner and Allan Gill looking for a route round a lead

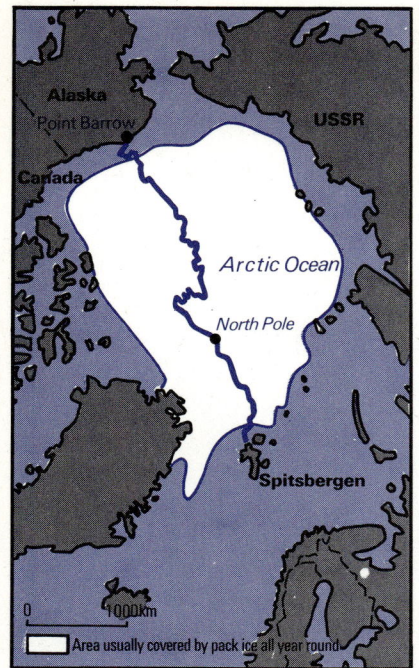

The British Trans-Arctic Expedition on top of the world — the North Pole

they continued their journey on 4 September. Four days later Allan Gill stumbled and fell. His injury, a slipped disc, meant that the team had to return to the ice floe where they had spent the previous two months. There they found a place to camp for the long, dark winter — a winter during which they worked fifteen hours a day collecting micro-meteorological, glaciological and geophysical data, but during which they also drifted 209 kilometres (130 miles) off course.

Almost a year after their departure from Point Barrow, the team was 563 kilometres (350 miles) behind schedule and barely half-way across the top of the world.

To reach their destination before the next summer melt they would have to complete the second half of their journey in a third of the time they had taken for the first half.

When the floe on which they were camped shattered on 24 February 1969, the team, navigating by Venus and the Moon, headed for the North Pole.

Because the ice is continually moving the exact position of the Pole is extremely difficult to find. Wally Herbert described trying to set foot on it as "like trying to step on the shadow of a bird that is circling overhead". Nevertheless they found it on 6 April — the first indisputable attainment of the North Pole by sledge.

The journey ahead of them seemed almost impossible to make in the time that remained. Travelling as light as possible, and taking no rest days except for those when further supplies were dropped, the team headed south (the only way you can travel from the North Pole) — their objective, Spitsbergen.

They averaged over 24 kilometres (15 miles) a day for a further sixty days, travelling at night when the ice was firm. Then their goal came into view — land — the first they had seen for nearly sixteen months

They had covered 5,820 route kilometres (3,616 route miles) When members of the team stepped onto a small rocky island at 1900 hours GMT on 29 May, they had completed the first sledge crossing of the Arctic Ocean, a journey which in both time and distance was the longest sustained journey in the history of polar exploration. At that moment the British Trans-Arctic Expedition felt "on top of the world" — even though they weren't any more !

"Fritz" Koerner and one of his dogs cross a giant lead in the pack ice by using a sledge wrapped in a tarpaulin

# TAKE NOTE !

That's part of our signature tune which has been played on every *Record Breakers* programme for the past four years. It's got a long way to go before it's as well known as this tune.

Our National Anthem isn't the oldest in the world. That record is held by "Kimigayo" of Japan in which the words date from the ninth century. "Kimigayo" together with the anthems of Jordan and San Marino are joint record holders for being the shortest anthems — they each consist of only four lines. Of course, that doesn't include the anthems of Bahrain and Qatar which have no words at all.

There is one record, however, that our National Anthem did create. On 9 February 1909, King Edward VII arrived by train at Rathenau railway station, Brandenburg, Germany. An official party was waiting on the platform to welcome him, and as the train drew to a halt a German military band struck up "God Save The King". Inside the train, His Majesty was still getting dressed in the uniform of a German Field Marshal. When he failed to appear, the band repeated the National Anthem. The King still did not appear — so the band repeated it again, and they continued to do so until His Majesty, correctly attired, alighted from the train.

No one is quite sure how many times the anthem was played, certainly sixteen times, maybe seventeen, but one thing is certain — it was the longest official rendering of a National Anthem ever to take place.

It must have been pretty monotonous too, for both officials and bandsmen alike, but not nearly as monotonous as a song called "Ein Ton" written by Peter Cornelius of Germany in 1859.

# Ein Ton.

„Mir klingt ein Ton so wunderbar."

Nr.12. Etwas bewegt.
*Poco mosso.*

Mir klingt ein Ton so wun-der-bar In Herz und
Sin-nen im-mer-dar. Ist es der
Hauch, der dir ent-schwebt, Als ein-mal noch dein Mund ge-bet?
Ist es des Glöckleins trü-ber Klang, Der dir ge-
folgt den Weg ent-lang? Mir klingt der
Ton so voll und rein, Als schlöß er dei-ne See-le ein,
Als stie-gest lie-bend nie-der
du Und sän-gest mei-nen Schmerz in Ruh!

The B above Middle C is repeated eighty times in twenty-nine bars.

Tastes in music vary widely and some people prefer more modern works. American John Cage wrote a work which, as can be seen from his handwritten score, is a "solo to be performed in any way by anyone". It is an opus called "4 Minutes 33 Seconds" and it is four minutes and

SOLO TO BE PERFORMED IN ANY WAY BY ANYONE

IN A SITUATION PROVIDED WITH MAXIMUM AMPLIFICATION (NO FEEDBACK), PERFORM A DISCIPLINED ACTION.

*John Cage*

thirty-three seconds of silence. After "hearing" it, Igor Stravinsky, the famous composer, said he looked forward to John Cage's next composition and hoped it would be "a work of a major length".

Unfortunately, Stravinsky died before being able to listen to "Auditory Memory", a work of a major length composed by American Jerry Cammarata in 1974.

"Auditory Memory" lasts fifty-two minutes and ten seconds — fifty-two minutes and ten seconds of silence. It has even been produced on a long-playing record in the United States. The obvious question the composer is always being asked is "why subject somebody to listening to nothing?"

Jerry answers: "There is a very important part of the brain that's rarely used. It's the auditory memory quartex. It's my belief more people should take an interest in it, because it's important to be able to sit down and conjure up in the mind all kinds of musical sounds. By putting my disc on your record player, you've got to use your brain and imagine the sounds. Some people have to be told to do that."

"Auditory Memory" 52:10

ad lib

fine

Jerry claims "Auditory Memory" is being used by some schools in the United States. He freely admits too, that he never thought of recording it in stereo or quadrophonic. That's a pity, because he also advises that you should listen to it on a good record player with the volume on full — "for total appreciation".

The longest silent musical composition in the world isn't Jerry's first taste of being a record breaker. He started back in June 1972 when he decided to break the marathon singing record of twenty-six hours fifteen minutes held by Tony Coleno of Cambridge.

As a speech pathologist and audiologist at a New York College, Cammarata was interested in how much punishment the vocal chords could stand. He took the world record to the United States by singing non-stop (except for the permitted five minutes' break every hour) for forty-eight hours, only to find the following year that the record was back in Britain. Between 18 and 21 June 1973, Eamon McGirr sang "Now is the Hour" and eighty-eight other community songs in Eccles, Lancashire, for an incredible seventy-two hours thirty-one minutes. Cammarata however was determined the record should reside in America and four weeks later, with a repertoire of nine hundred and seventeen songs, went on for seventy-five hours — this time doing it all in a bath !

Cammarata versus . . .

. . . McGirr

McGirr was just as determined the record should stay on this side of the Atlantic, and regained the title with a virtually unbelievable one hundred and five hours at Stalybridge in Manchester on 5-10 August 1974. What did that make Cammarata do ? "I'll think about it".

Two years later he's still thinking about it, but who knows. Maybe at the very moment you're reading this . . .

# IT'S ALL RIGHT FOR SUM!

Try this on your friends. Ask them to choose any number from 1 to 9. Multiply the number by 9. Multiply the result by the numbers 1 to 9 excluding 8. i.e. 1 2 3 4 5 6 7 9. The answer will be a row of the first number chosen. Here's an example : Suppose the number chosen is 4.

Multiply it by 9    $9 \times 4 = 36$
Multiply 36 by 1 2 3 4 5 6 7 9

```
    1 2 3 4 5 6 7 9
              3 6
  ─────────────────
    7 4 0 7 4 0 7 4
  3 7 0 3 7 0 3 7 0
  ─────────────────
Answer : 4 4 4 4 4 4 4 4 4
```

If that's too difficult, here's another one :

Multiply 111, 111, 111 by
111, 111, 111
The answer is :
12345678987654321

For centuries mathematicians have amused themselves with tricks like those and a favourite pastime was contriving "Magic" squares.

| 16 | 3 | 2 | 13 |
|----|----|----|----|
| 5 | 10 | 11 | 8 |
| 9 | 6 | 7 | 12 |
| 4 | 15 | 14 | 1 |

This one is so arranged that vertical, horizontal and diagonal rows add up to 34.

The four middle boxes also total 34 as do the four corners. It was created and incorporated into an engraving called "Melancholia" by the German painter Albrecht Dürer. In the two centre boxes on the bottom row, he also included the year he completed it – 1514.

Dürer's magic square was simpler than one created by the eighteenth-century mathematician Leonard Euler.

Horizontally or vertically each row totals 260, each half row 130 ; but even more astounding is the fact that a chess knight, starting from number 1 and making its L-shaped moves, can land on all 64 boxes in numerical order.

Another intriguing square is one created by Benjamin Franklin, the famous printer, publisher, author, inventor, scientist and diplomat who two hundred years ago helped to frame the American Declaration of Independence.

Like Dürer's square, each row horizontally and vertically adds up to 260. Tracing a diagonal up four boxes and down four boxes also totals 260, as does the four corners plus the four boxes in the middle. Each half row totals 130 as does the sum of the numbers in any four-box sub-square. Any four numbers that lie diametrically equidistant from the centre also total 130.

To check all three magic squares needs only simple addition, but in higher mathematics such as calculus, things become a little more complex.

This photograph of Roy with a mirror, taken in a mirror, shows his image reflected over and over, each one getting smaller and smaller, ad infinitum.

Theoretically, it is impossible to calculate how many images there are, and in circumstances like these, mathematicians would use "convergence to a limit" — a

| 52 | 61 | 4  | 13 | 20 | 29 | 36 | 45 |
| 14 | 3  | 62 | 51 | 46 | 35 | 30 | 19 |
| 53 | 60 | 5  | 12 | 21 | 28 | 37 | 44 |
| 11 | 6  | 59 | 54 | 43 | 38 | 27 | 22 |
| 55 | 58 | 7  | 10 | 23 | 26 | 39 | 42 |
| 9  | 8  | 57 | 56 | 41 | 40 | 25 | 24 |
| 50 | 63 | 2  | 15 | 18 | 31 | 34 | 47 |
| 16 | 1  | 64 | 49 | 48 | 33 | 32 | 17 |

fundamental concept of calculus using the idea that an unknown value can be measured by "closing in" through approximations that are finer and finer, until in effect, they are refined to a precise value.

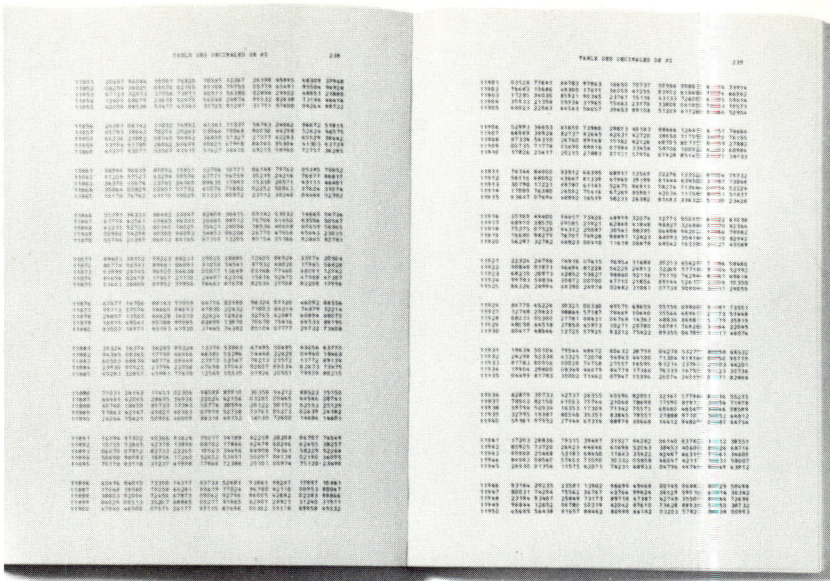

The world's most boring book ?

Probably the best known example of convergence is contained in a book by the French mathematicians Jean Guilland and Martine Bouyer. On 24 May 1973, using a CDC 7600 computer, they calculated pi ($\pi$ — the ratio of any circle's circumference to its diameter) to one million decimal places. The answer occupies four hundred pages in what has been described as the world's most boring book.

Memorising pi as well as calculating it to a great number of decimal places is difficult because there is no logical relationship in the sequence of numbers, but on 15 October 1974, Michael John Poulteney BA (Oxon) of Bede Sixth Form College, Billingham, Cleveland, England, did manage to recite it from memory to 3,025 decimal places. He could not remember the 3,026th place which is, of course, zero.

Not all mathematical problems involve pi of course. This one doesn't.

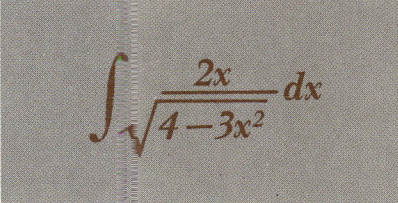

$$\int \frac{2x}{\sqrt{4-3x^2}}\,dx$$

It's an integral calculus problem, the type you wouldn't normally start doing at school until you're about sixteen years of age. But on television in Tokyo on 2 November 1967, this problem was set by Professor Yano, Professor of Mathematics at the Tokyo Institute of Technology, for Kim Ung-Yong of Seoul, South Korea, to solve. He did it without any trouble even though he was only four years and eight months old – at that age a feat of supreme intelligence.

On the Terman index for Intelligence Quotients, 150 represents "genius" level, and many people hold the view that indices over 200 are immeasurable. Nevertheless, a figure of 210 has been attributed to Kim Ung-Yong, who, before he was five years old, could not only do integral calculus, but also write poetry and speak four languages: English, German, Japanese, and Korean.

His parents, Dr and Mrs Kim Soo Sun, were both born at 11 am on 23 May 1934. Whether that has anything to do with the fact that Kim is a genius no one is quite sure. But the fact that they are also both professors at a University and used to take Kim along with them to study physics, philosophy and maths when he was too young to attend school, must have helped. Well, if the opportunity knocked at your door, wouldn't you? Well, wouldn't you?

Joe Davis

One of the most popular programmes on television is ''Pot Black'' – where the world's finest professional snooker players demonstrate their skill with such accuracy they make playing the game seem positively simple – which it isn't.

Invented by Field-Marshal Sir Neville Chamberlain in India over one hundred years ago, snooker was first played in England in 1885. Fourteen years later the modern scoring system was adopted, since when snooker has increased in popularity so much that today it is played nearly all over the world.

The table used is a bed of slate 365.7 cms long by 186.7 cms wide (12' x 6' 1½''), which is covered with green woollen cloth. Rubber cushions surround the table which has a pocket at each of the four corners and one in the centre of each long side.

Twenty-two balls, all the same size and weight, are used in the game. Fifteen are red and score one point each. The ''colours'' as they are called, consist of one yellow which scores two, one green which scores three, one brown which scores four, one blue which scores five, one pink which scores six and one black which scores seven.

The white ball, called the cue ball, is struck with a cue. Each player takes his turn at the table, the object being to pot all the ''reds'' and ''colours'' into any of the six pockets. This can only be done, however, in the following way.

One player tries to pot a red ball. If he succeeds, he can try and pot any ''colour'' of his choice. If that is successful, he must pot another red before potting another colour, continuing until he misses. When a red goes into a pocket it is left there, but each time a colour is potted it is put back on the table on its own spot.

When all fifteen reds have

# THE POT

Rex Williams

been disposed of, the colours must then be potted in this order: yellow, green, brown, blue, pink, and black. This time each colour that is potted stays in the pocket.

The player who has scored most points at the end of the game, or "frame", as it is called, is the winner.

Excluding handicaps or penalties, the maximum score any player can make in one turn at the table is a hundred and forty-seven points – fifteen reds, each followed by the black, followed by all the colours. This has only been achieved twice in official competitions in the history of snooker.

At the Leicester Square Hall, London, on 22 January 1955, Joe Davis, OBE, did it while playing against Willie Smith. Over ten years later, on 22 December 1965, Rex Williams also achieved it against Manuel Francisco in Cape Town, South Africa.

All snooker matches are played on a "billiards" table. Billiards is a similar, but more difficult, game using only three balls – two white and one red.

Before the 1930s snooker was played by professional billiards' players only for fun. The man who made a study of the use of billiard-shot technique in snooker was the

legendary Joe Davis. It was he, more than anyone else, who turned snooker into a game of supreme skill which today has achieved its own status.

Joe Davis, undefeated world snooker champion for twenty years, proved, by winning seven United Kingdom and four World Billiards titles, that nearly all the best snooker players are also brilliant billiard players. It's not surprising therefore to find that Rex Williams, the only other official record breaker for the maximum break in snooker, is, and has been since 1968, World Professional Billiards Champion.

# RECORD RECORDS

The BBC holds more records than anyone else in the world – about one million of them. They are the gramophone type of course, and they make up the biggest gramophone library in the world, a library that exists for the sole purpose of supplying records for the hundreds of BBC radio and television programmes that are broadcast every week.

Among those one million records are some which are record records. On one shelf there's the Beatles "I Want to Hold Your Hand" – the top-selling British record of all-time. On another, the aria "Vesti la giubba" from the opera *I Pagliacci* sung by the Italian tenor Enrico Caruso – the earliest recording to sell one million copies.

Elsewhere in the library there are recordings made by Miss Lata Mangeshker, who since 1948 has recorded over 25,000 solo, duet and chorus backed songs in twenty Indian languages, and in another place is an LP called "John Fitzgerald Kennedy – A Memorial Album". Recorded on 22 November 1963, the day President Kennedy was assassinated, it sold four million copies in just six days.

If you like buying LPs, you'd no doubt like to know the longest long-playing set of discs ever sold. It's the "Complete Works of William Shakespeare" recorded by the Argo Record Company. It costs £409.63 to buy which is a lot of money, but you get a lot for it – one hundred and thirty-seven LPs that give one hundred and thirty hours' listening time. That's a great deal longer than the smallest record in the world. Made by HMV Record Company in 1924, the record is 3.5 centimetres (1⅜ inches) in diameter, and is a recording of "God Save the King".

Only two hundred and fifty of these records were produced so they're extremely rare. But not as rare as the BBC Gramophone Library's most valued possession. It's a disc of "The Lord's Prayer" spoken by Emile Berliner.

Berliner was the man who invented the disc record-player. He applied for a patent for his "gramophone" on 26 September 1887 and gave a demonstration of the apparatus at the Franklin Institute Philadelphia, on 16 May 1888. The hand-cranked machine played a 127 millimetre (5 inch) rubber disc at a speed of about 70 r.p.m. The first recording he made on the gramophone was of himself reciting "The Lord's Prayer" – the world's first disc.

Even though the BBC Gramophone Library has a lot of records and quite a few record records, the forty-five members of staff who run it insist that they themselves are not record breakers – in any way!

The actual size of the world's smallest record

The Berliner gramophone

Queen Elizabeth II

King Faisal
of Saudi Arabia

King Constantine
of Greece

King Peter II
of Yugoslavia

Queen Juliana
of the Netherlands

King Hussein
of Jordan

King Mahendra Bin Bikram
Shahdera of Nepal

King Frederick IX
of Denmark

King Umberto II
of Italy

What have all these people got in common — apart from the fact that they are or were kings or queens? The answer is, when they visited New York they all stayed in

# THE WALDORF ASTORIA

The Waldorf Astoria is the largest commercial hotel in the world. One hundred and twenty-three and a half metres long by sixty-one metres wide, and forty-seven stories high, it contains one thousand nine hundred bedrooms – each with a private bath, air-conditioning, telephone, and colour television. Every room also has a radio on which guests can tune to the world's largest hotel radio-receiving system. One thousand seven hundred staff are needed to run the hotel, which spends £10,000 a year on light bulbs and has an annual electricity bill of over a million pounds. Fifty thousand sheets are laundered every week and the hotel consumes half a million gallons of water every day. If these facts are difficult to believe, there are some even stranger ones:

Two men do nothing all day
except break non-returnable
bottles — ten thousand of them.

Another man does nothing all
day except squeeze oranges —
four thousand of them.

And yet another does nothing all
day except make coffee — one
thousand gallons of it.

Two ladies do nothing all day
except crawl around on their
knees inspecting the carpets for
holes — and mending them.

The hotel kitchens prepare over three million meals every year and they'll cook whatever the guests request – and that includes fried ice cream.

Their dishwashing machines wash half a million different pieces of crockery every day – which isn't all that surprising when you realise that it's quite common for the hotel to serve six thousand breakfasts all at the same time and on the same evening cope with ten thousand dinners.

Chef Arno Schmidt, inventor of fried ice-cream

For New Yorkers who want a grand party, the Waldorf Astoria is the hotel they choose – because it's been famous for them for years.

But the most famous one of all took place on 10 February 1897. It was given by a Mr and Mrs Bradley Martin who had just returned to New York from a two-year trip to the continent.

Mrs Martin, whose father had left her six million dollars, was a bit of a social climber and she was determined to rock the city with the most glittering ball it had ever seen.

Seven hundred and fifty of the "very best people" were invited – all in fancy dress of English, French and German history of the 16th to 18th centuries.

The furniture was entirely Louis XV – two hundred policemen supervised the guest arrivals – and not only were there no flowers left in New York, but others were brought in from Boston and Philadelphia. The musicians' balcony was covered in pink roses – in February !

It was a party that caused a sensation – and the bill was sensational too. It cost three hundred and sixty-nine thousand, two hundred dollars in the days when dollars were made of solid gold. That's equivalent to two million pounds today. It's the most expensive private party that's ever been held.

If experts throughout the world were asked whom they consider to be the greatest athlete of the century, the man who would almost certainly get more votes than all the other contenders put together is American Jesse Owens.

Known as "The Ebony Antelope", his scintillating performances became the historic centrepiece of the 1936 Olympic Games in Berlin — performances which will never be forgotten by all who had the privilege of seeing them.

On the first day of the Games, 2 August, he equalled the Olympic 100-metres record in 10.3 seconds in the first round, and improved it to 10.2 seconds in the quarter-final. This time, equal to the world record, could not be accepted as such however, because of wind assistance.

One day later, after a leisurely semi-final in 10.4 seconds, Owens again equalled the Olympic record of 10.3 seconds in the final — and won his first gold medal. On the third day, in each of the first two rounds of the 200-metres, Owens broke the Olympic record with a time of 21.2 seconds. He then took time off from sprinting to win a second gold medal in the long jump — and break another games record with a leap of 8.06 metres (26′ 5¼″).

The following day, 5 August, saw him back on the track in the semi-final and final of the 200-metres — winning yet another gold medal and, with a time of 20.7 seconds, breaking yet another Olympic record.

After a two-day rest, he was back in action again, this time helping the American team to victory in the 4 × 100-metres relay. They equalled the world record of 40.0 seconds in the heat and set a new one of 39.8 seconds in the final the following day. That was Jesse Owens' final achievement in an Olympic Games in which he had run and won ten races, gained four gold medals and equalled or broken twelve Olympic records.

Those performances gave Owens world-wide fame and a hero's welcome on his return to the United States — a far cry from his childhood.

The second youngest of eleven children, he was born on 12 September 1913 at Danville, Alabama — the son of Emma and James Cleveland Owens. His father was a cotton field cropper and like thousands of other negro families of the deep south, the Owens were poor, so poor that none of the children had any shoes.

Jesse Owens setting the world long-jump record that stood for over a quarter of a century

In 1920, the family moved to Cleveland, Ohio, so that his father could work as a labourer in a factory. It was there that the seven-year-old entered a brick building for the first time in his life — a school. On being asked his name by the teacher, he replied: "J.C. Owens, Ma'am." The teacher wrote down "Jesse Owens". He's been Jesse Owens ever since. While still at school, his natural ability for running was spotted by an Irish immigrant called Charley Riley, who was the physical education instructor at a nearby high school. But it wasn't only Owens' natural ability that impressed Riley — it was his dedication and willingness to learn.

Riley taught him to run as if he had a glass of water on his head, and to imagine the track was a bed of hot coals: "Leave your feet on the ground for too long and they're going to get burnt." Commenting on his style years later, one sports critic wrote: "You never seemed to see his feet coming down at all. They always seemed to be leaving the track."

By the time he was fifteen years old, Jesse could run the 100-yards in 9.8 seconds, long jump nearly 23 feet and high jump 6 feet.

A few years later he helped his school win the National Championships. He'd competed in the sprints, hurdles and long jump, but hit the headlines by equalling the world record in the 100-yards — as a nineteen-year-old schoolboy. When the team arrived back in Cleveland, they were given a civic reception, but that didn't help his family very much. With the great depression on and his father out of work, Jesse had to earn money to help pay his family's rent.

Approached by twenty-eight Universities who wanted him to run for them, Jesse picked the Ohio State University, the only one that also offered him a job — as a lift boy in the Ohio House of Representatives.

For the next three years, he studied all day, worked all evening, and trained whenever there was a spare moment with his coach Larry Snyder. His sights were set on the Berlin Olympic Games in 1936. It was those years of work that ended with his four Olympic gold medals. But like all Olympic gold medals, they are there to be won. That's not to say winning one is easy, but it's easier than breaking a world record. Although "The Ebony Antelope" will always be remembered for his performances in the Berlin Olympics, his greatest efforts were in fact achieved a year earlier.

He was competing for the Ohio State University in the Big Ten College Championships held at Ann Arbor, Michigan. Having fallen down some stairs two weeks earlier, he arrived at the track in such pain that Larry Snyder suggested he ought to scratch rather than risk doing his back any further damage. Jesse said he'd try the 100-yards to see how his back stood up to the strain. At 3.15 pm after needing help to get his track suit off, he came under the starter's orders. When the gun went off, the pain went and so did Jesse Owens — he equalled the world record of 9.4 seconds. Ten minutes later in the long jump, Owens waited on the runway for his first attempt. Someone optimistically had placed a white handkerchief in the sand at the world record mark set by the Japanese jumper Chuhei Nambu in Tokyo four years earlier. Owens flashed down the runway and took off. He landed almost six inches past the handkerchief, setting a new world record of 8.13 metres ($26'8\frac{1}{4}''$) — a record that was to stand for over twenty-five years.

Wanting some more points for his team, Larry Snyder withdrew Owens from the long jump after his single effort so that he could run in the 220-yards, due to start a few minutes later.

The gun cracked, Owens flashed, and the timekeepers blinked. Their watches had stuttered to a halt at 20.3 seconds – 0.3 seconds faster than the world record that was set nine years earlier. Since the record for the slightly shorter 200-metres also stood at 20.6 seconds, Owens collected not one, but two world records for the one race.

Yet that was still not the end. Fifteen minutes later he was in action again, this time in the 220-yards low hurdles. He broke the tape in yet another world record time – 22.6 seconds. Once again, as both the previous 220-yards and 200-metres low hurdles record had been 23.0 seconds, Owens captured both.

So it was that on Saturday, 25 May 1935, Jesse Owens, "The Ebony Antelope", set *six* world records in less than one hour – a unique and amazing achievement that will remain forever in the history books of the athletic world.

# DID YOU KNOW...

. . . that during his lifetime, sexton Johann Heinrich Karl Thieme of Aldenburg, Germany, dug 23,311 graves!

. . . that on 17 October 1971 Frank Freer (USA) spent eight hours peeling an apple 38 cms (15 ins) in circumference to get a single unbroken peel that measured 39.86 m (130 ft 8½ ins)

# WHAT'S IN A FACE?

In February 1959, in a small town just outside Los Angeles in California, the owner of a jewellery shop was just shutting up for the night when a late customer rushed in and asked if he could buy an engagement ring. The jeweller, only too happy to oblige, had just produced a tray of rings, when he found himself looking straight down the muzzle of a sawn-off shotgun. After locking the jeweller in his own vault, the thief set the alarm system so that the police would think the shop was closed up for the night and walked off with over £10,000 worth of jewellery.

Three hours later, in a town fifty miles away, he was arrested by a police officer, despite the fact that he had no criminal record and had worn gloves, therefore leaving no fingerprints. How did it happen?

After the jeweller had released himself and phoned the police, a detective arrived at the shop with a small wooden box. Inside were five hundred and thirty-six photographic transparencies called ''foils'' – one hundred and thirty different hairlines, thirty-seven kinds of noses, one hundred and twenty types of eyes, fifty-two shapes of chin, forty sets of lips, and various types of eyebrows, beards, moustaches, wrinkles, glasses and hats. Enough different combinations to reproduce a strong likeness of nearly sixty-two billion people – more than walk on the face of the earth.

While the jeweller described the different

features of the thief's face, the detective laid foil on top of foil until a likeness had been produced. That facial description of a criminal and his subsequent arrest by Sheriff Peter J. Pitchess, was the first time ever that Identikit, as that small box is called, was used in apprehending a criminal.

Identikit was invented by Hugh C. McDonald, a detective who was transferred to the Identification Bureau of the Los Angeles County Sheriff's Department.

While working with endless fingerprint files, he came up with the idea that if fingerprints, with their billions of possible combinations, could be precisely described by letters and numbers, the same ought to be possible with people's heads and faces. He spent year after year after year of painstaking work on the project. Fifty thousand pictures of faces were dissected, analysed measured and compared. Then, after a series of selective experiments, he produced a master set from which every one of the fifty thousand original photographs taken could be recognisably reproduced by the correct combination of the six basic features: nose, lips, eyes, chin, eyebrows and hair. Master foils were made and Identikit had been invented.

On a recent visit to the Los Angeles County Sheriff's Department, Roy Castle took the opportunity to describe someone he knew to Deputy Frederica Davis, an Identikit expert who, not knowing he was describing Norris McWhirter, started the test by making a few notes in order to get a general description of the person. These included the sex, age, height, weight, colour of hair and eyes, and any distinguishing features such as scars, beard, moustache, glasses etc.

It was only at this point that Deputy Davis started to build up an Identikit picture, using a book of the various outlines for Roy to choose from.

She started with the hair, and Roy chose a receding hairline. Deputy Davis selected the foil that had the same number as the drawing and placed it on a metal base plate. So, with Roy choosing the drawings and Deputy Davis selecting the appropriate foils, a face was gradually built up that had "kindish" eyes, a "sharpish" nose, a "thin" mouth and "fairly slim" eyebrows.

On looking at the complete Identikit picture Roy was unhappy about the hair – it was too dark. This was corrected by Deputy Davis using two grease pencils – a black one, just to lengthen the sideburns, and a white one, to lighten the hair and the eyebrows.

"That's coming on fine," said Roy, "but the face looks a bit sour – it should be slightly happier." Deputy Davis explained that what they were aiming for was a general

likeness, not a photograph. "On the whole, Roy, criminals are not seen smiling! However, all the foils have several notches at the side so I'll try moving the chin up a bit to shorten it and make him look less severe."

In normal circumstances, once an Identikit picture is completed it is copied on a special photostat machine and distributed in the area where the crime took place so that police and the general public can be on the lookout for the criminal. Because each foil is numbered, the components of the Identikit picture, together with information about the crime, can also be sent to any police force in the world that has an Identikit box, and they can make up a duplicate.

As a special favour, Deputy Davis also made up an Identikit picture of Roy – but promised she would not send the details to Scotland Yard!

# MAY I HAVE THE PLEASURE?

In classical ballet the greatest number of consecutive spins is the thirty-two *fouettés rond de jambe en tournant* in Tchaikovsky's "Swan Lake". During this movement, performed *sur la pointe*, the working leg never touches the floor. In 1940, in Melbourne, Australia, Rowena Jackson, MBE, achieved one hundred and twenty-one consecutive turns in her ballet class. *Fouettés* are performed by ballerinas – but there is also a record-breaking ballet step for men.

It's called an *entrechat* – a vertical jump starting and finishing in the fifth position. While the dancer is in the air with his legs extended, he criss-crosses them at the lower calf before landing.

The great Russian dancer, Vaslav Nijinsky, born in 1890, was reputedly the only man ever to have performed an *entrechat dix* – that is crossing and uncrossing the legs four times – the starting and finishing position each counting as one.

But on 7 January 1973, Royal Ballet Principal Dancer Wayne Sleep came on *The Record Breakers* to try and beat it.

After the jump was completed, it was analysed in slow motion and proved to be an *entrechat douze*. That means Wayne crossed and uncrossed his legs five times while performing this difficult step. He was in the air for just 0.71 of a second.

One week later on the programme Roy Castle also claimed a dancing record, this time for tap. Using a digital counter that registered sound beats through a microphone, Roy was measured at twenty-four taps per second, or one thousand four hundred and forty per minute. He used a step that gave five beats on each foot – and he's a fast foot-tapping Record Breaker!

# ITCHY FEET

The person who can claim to have the "itchiest feet" in the world is Jesse Hart Rosdail. Born in 1914 in Elmhurst, Illinois, in the United States, he was twenty years old when he decided he'd like to see Europe. To do so, he bought a fifty-year-old German bicycle and pedalled 17,703 kilometres (11,000 miles) round it.

He enjoyed that trip so much he followed it by taking his bicycle to Africa, clocked up another 18,668 kilometres (11,600 miles) and followed *that* by pedalling round Australia for six months. Since then, Jesse has travelled and travelled, alone, to two hundred and eighty-six different countries. He's the most travelled man on earth, and to date has nearly two and a half million kilometres (one and a half million miles) behind him. North Korea, North Vietnam, China, Cuba and French Antarctic Territories are the only countries he hasn't visited, but he's hoping to do those one day to complete the list.

Jesse is a teacher, and when the school holidays come around he just "packs a bag" and takes off. "Packing a bag" is simple for him because no matter where he goes he takes just one small holdall. It contains a towel, soap, hair-oil, a rain-suit, bathing-suit, a shirt, a camera and a tent that can also be used as a sleeping bag — a total weight of just over seven kilogrammes (eighteen pounds). He also carries his passport — his seventh since he took his first trip. All of them have additional pages stuck in to cope with the visas, entry and exit stamps he's collected during his travels — nearly a thousand of them.

Crown Range, New Zealand, 1947

Out of all the places he's visited, the country he likes best is New Zealand, "a country with a happy combination of Swiss mountains and Norwegian fiords — snow scenes and waterfalls — white sheep on green hillsides — beautiful trees and friendly people."

The contact with people is one of the main aspects of Jesse's trips. He's stayed or eaten in eight hundred and sixty-nine different homes in almost every country he's visited. This is a contributing factor to why he's been able to make so many journeys at such small cost. But he doesn't mind roughing it either — and loves to sleep out in the desert miles from anywhere.

For someone with his experience, you'd expect Jesse to be a good traveller. He is on the whole, but he has experienced some difficulties. In 1973 he chartered a small boat to try and reach some reefs near the Friendly Isles of Tonga. They set off in what Jesse described as "a tub if ever I saw one" and hit heavy seas. In such a small boat, which was being tossed all over the place, it was impossible to stand up, so Jesse took refuge in the hold which was only four feet high. Together with the rest of the crew and some smelly, squashed bananas, he spent three days getting soaked to the skin by heavy waves that were pounding over the boat. Jesse remarked at the time: "It's at a time like this that you really have to tell yourself that you love travel."

Like most travellers though there's one place Jesse Hart Rosdail likes to go more than anywhere else in the world — and that's home. "Pretty good place, you know".

Potential record breakers please note. At the present time there are only a hundred and fifty-nine sovereign and sixty-four non-sovereign territories left in the world — a total of two hundred and twenty-three.

# DID YOU KNOW...

. . . THAT "THE SIXTH SICK SHEIK'S SIXTH SHEEP'S SICK!"
(Try saying it fast)

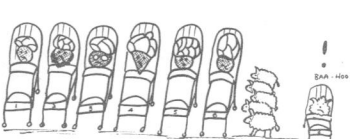

. . . that a hailstone weighing 750 grams (1.67 lbs.), with a diameter of 19 cms ($7\frac{1}{2}$ ins) and a circumference of 44.45 cms ($17\frac{1}{2}$ ins) was found at Coffeyville, Kansas, USA on 3 September 1970!

# DID YOU KNOW...

. . . that in February 1964, at an auction in Hollywood, California, USA, a woman bought a piece of land measuring 7.6 x 16.5 x 14.6 cms (3 x 6½ x 5½ ins) and paid $510 (£212.50) for it!

The most expensive piece of land in the world

# ON THE UP

If there's one thing that can be said to be "on the up and up" it's the world's structures. Office blocks, flats, hotels, chimneys, towers and television masts are built taller and taller almost every year.

On Manhattan Island, New York City, where civil engineers have no choice but to build upwards because of lack of space, there's an office block at the junction of Fifth Avenue with Broadway and 23rd Street. Built in 1902 by Daniel H. Burnham, it's 91.44 metres (300 feet) tall, has twenty-one storeys, and is known as the Flat-iron building.

Since then it has been dwarfed by hundreds of buildings. For thirty-nine years the world's tallest building was Manhattan's Empire State, completed on 1 May 1931 at a cost of seventeen million pounds. It's got six thousand five hundred windows, three and a half thousand miles of telephone wires, sixty miles of water pipe and it's 448 metres (1,472 feet) high. One thousand eight hundred and sixty steps have to be climbed to reach floor one hundred and two – the top. But luckily, there are also seventy-three lifts.

Today, the tallest building record is held by the Sears Tower, headquarters of Sears Roebuck Company, the department stores. Located in Wacker Drive, Chicago, Illinois, it was completed on 4 May 1973. It was designed by Fazlur R. Khan, who was born in Dacca and studied engineering in Calcutta. Khan was the first engineer to use a new concept of "tubular building" – a concept that was economical in the use of steel, and which therefore made dramatic savings in the structural costs of very tall buildings. The Sears Tower is a marvellous example of his work – nine square tubes,

Flat-iron building

Empire State Building

Sears Tower
Chicago
548.64 metres (1,800 feet)

Empire State Building
New York City
448 metres (1,472 feet)

Post Office Tower
London
188.9 metres (620 feet)

Flat-iron Building
New York City
91.44 metres (300 feet)

**Warszawa Mast**
Plock Poland
645.38 metres (2,117 feet)

**CN Tower**
Toronto
533.33 metres (1,815 feet)

bundled together in threes to form a square. Each tube is a different height, the tallest rising to 443 metres (1,454 feet) – that's well over a quarter of a mile. Sixteen thousand five hundred people use the building every day, and they can reach any of the hundred and ten floors by using one of the hundred and three lifts or eighteen escalators. On top of the building are two television masts which make the absolute height 548.64 metres (1,800 feet), but these are not the tallest TV masts in the world.

That record goes to the Warszawa mast at Konstantynow near Plock in Poland. Designed by Jan Polack, it's built of tubular galvanised steel, weighs 558 tonnes (550 tons) and is 645.38 metres (2,117 feet 4$\frac{1}{2}$ inches) tall – so tall, that if anyone had the misfortune to fall off the top, they would have the consolation of knowing that they would reach their terminal velocity – 53.64 metres per second (120 miles per hour) –

and cease to be accelerating before they hit the ground! Completed on 18 May 1974, the mast is not self-supporting, ie it is kept upright by fifteen steel guy ropes. The world's tallest free-standing tower is the CN Tower in Metro Centre, Toronto, Canada. Work on the tower began on 12 February 1973 and went on for over two years – until 2 April 1975. In that time one hundred and thirty-two thousand tonnes (one hundred and thirty thousand tons) of reinforced, post-tensioned concrete were used in the building, which rises to 533.33 metres (1,815 feet 5 inches). From the revolving restaurant in the ''Sky Pod'' situated 347.5 metres (1,140 feet) above the ground it's possible, on a clear day, to see a distance of 120 kilometres (74$\frac{1}{2}$ miles).

First reports from people visiting the restaurant indicated that the food served there was of the highest quality – only, by the time they got round to eating it was cold – they were too busy looking at the view!

Sears Tower

CN Tower

# AS LIGHT AS A...

The world's smallest bird is Helena's humming bird. Found in Cuba and the Isle of Pines, an average male adult is just 58 millimetres (2.28 inches) in length. It weighs less than a Sphinx moth – about 2 grams (.07 oz.).

"As light as a breast feather of an Helena's humming bird."

On *The Record Breakers* in January 1973, we weighed something even lighter than that – the weight of the ink in a full stop like this . To do so we used a Q01 quartz-fibre decimicro balance – the finest balance in the world. The full stop weighed just 0.0000006 of a gram.

Records, however, are there to be broken and this one is no exception. An even finer balance is now being manufactured in Göttingen, West Germany. The new fine balance record holder is the Sartorius Model 4108 which can weigh to an accuracy of 0.01 micrograms or 0.00000001 of a gram.

Called an electronic vacuum ultra micro balance, it's used in research laboratories for measuring such things as corrosion, surface tension, gas chromatography, specific gravities, decomposition, sedimentations, vapour pressures and force and torque.

Measurements can be taken in any type of gas or controlled atmosphere, or even in a vacuum with this machine. So no matter what you care to put on the end of "As light as a . . .", the Sartorius 4108 will be able to tell you just how light it really is!

Weighing a full stop using the Q01 quartz-fibre decimicro balance

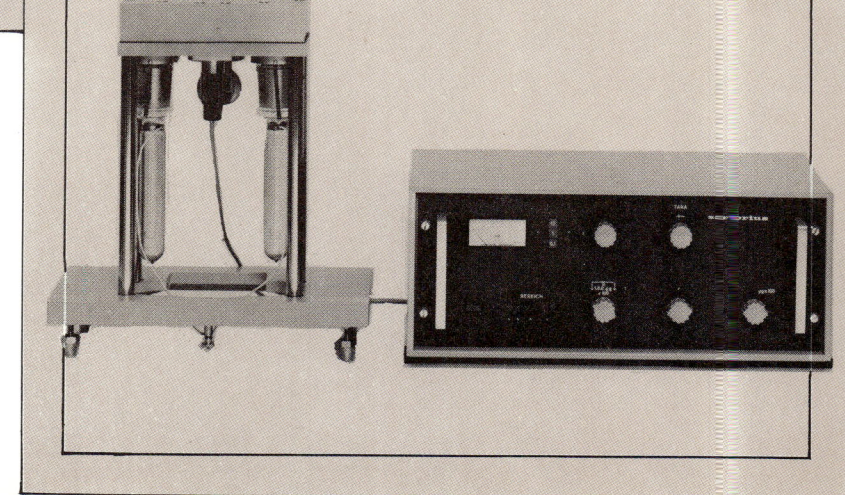

The Sartorius 4108

# AS SLIPPERY AS...

Most people finish that saying with the words "an eel". But should they?

During the Second World War, it became urgent to find new chemical materials which were needed to handle highly corrosive products used in the preparation of Uranium 235. A group of plastics known as fluorocarbon polymers were produced, among which was one named polytetrafluoroethylene. It's called PTFE for short and has a chemical formula $(C_2F_4)_n$.

The properties of polytetrafluoroethylene are outstanding.

1. It's virtually immune from chemical attack, being affected only by molten alkali metals and a few fluorine compounds at elevated temperatures.

2. It has a much wider working temperature range than any other plastic : from about $-196°C$ (the temperature of liquid nitrogen) to $+250°C$.

3. It's power factor and permittivity are both very low making it one of the best solid dielectrics known.

4. It cannot be wetted by water, nor can it absorb any, which, together with its high break-down voltage, make it an excellent electrical insulator.

5. It has the lowest coefficients of static and dynamic friction of any man-made solid – .02.

If you find the above technical jargon confusing, don't worry. Just remember that PTFE, manufactured in the United Kingdom by ICI and sold under the trade name "Fluon", is the world's most slippery substance – like wet ice on wet ice.

You've probably got a non-stick frying pan in your kitchen that's coated with it.

One more thing – the next time you hear the saying "As slippery as . . ." just add the word that should be at the end – "polytetrafluoroethylene".

Roy Castle attempting to walk up a 1 in 24 incline of polished steel wearing football boots with polytetrafluoroethylene studs. He didn't make it !

# THE FASTEST GUN IN THE WEST

Wyatt Earp

Doc Holliday

On 26 October 1881 at the back of the OK Corral in the town of Tombstone, Arizona, City Marshal Virgil Earp, together with his brothers Wyatt and Morgan and a friend called Doc Holliday, stood facing four cowboys. They were Ike and Billy Clanton, and Tom and Frank McLaury.

Billy drew his pistol and levelled it at Wyatt Earp. Wyatt ignored it, whipped out a six-shooter and fired at Frank. Less than a minute later, Billy

Clanton and both the McLaury brothers were dead. Virgil Earp had a bullet in his calf, Doc Holliday had one in the hip and Morgan Earp had one in the shoulder. Ike Clanton had run off. Only Wyatt Earp had come out unscathed in the most notorious shoot-out in the history of the West — the gun-fight at the OK Corral.

In those early days of the West, the law was the gun. Good and bad lived by it — or died by it. Sheriffs and horse thieves alike were all gun-fighters, and those that lived longest were those who could draw quickest.

Apart from the Earps, many other famous names have found their way into the gun-fight history books. Billy the Kid, who, by the age of twenty-one, boasted the fact that he had killed that number of men — twenty-one. Then there was George Parker and Harry Longbaugh, otherwise known as Butch Cassidy and the Sundance Kid. There was Jesse James and his equally lethal brother Frank, and there was also Wild Bill (James Butler) Hickok and Buffalo Bill Cody. Much has

been written about all of them, how accurate they were and how fast they were. But in the battle of the OK Corral, between thirty and forty shots were needed to kill three men at close range — as close as six feet ! Wyatt Earp considered Wild Bill Hickok to be the greatest marksman he had ever seen — able to shoot a cork through a bottle. Others regarded Wyatt himself as the fastest draw and shoot — particularly against a man who could shoot back !

Butch Cassidy . . .

. . . and the Sundance Kid

Despite legends that surround the names of people who have at sometime or another been labelled "The fastest gun in the West", it is doubtful if any of them could match the quick-draw champion of today — Bob Munden.

Born on 3 February 1942 in Kansas City, Missouri, Bob holds all the single-shot pistol records which, now the West has been won, are electronically timed under the rules of the International Fast-gun League. For obvious reasons of safety, the rules are very strict. Only single-action revolvers of .38 calibre or larger are permitted, and the gun must be a "real" one. The definition of a real gun is "one that weighs at least 963.8 gms (34 oz.), has a minimum barrel length of 117.5 mm. (4⅝ inches) and is capable of shooting a sustained amount of fully charged live ammunition."

Holsters too have their restrictions. They must be made from leather and cover seventy-five per cent of the gun's cylinder and all the barrel. They are not allowed to swivel or break open, and must not slant more than 45° from the ground.

Three main events are used in fast-draw competitions. The first, designed to resemble a man-to-man gun-fight of the old West days, is "Walk and Draw Level Blanks".

In this contest, two men walk towards each other. Between them is a light operated by the referee. When the light goes on, the two men draw and fire — blanks of course. An electronic clock, automatically started when the "draw" light is switched on, is stopped by the noise of the gun. It also indicates which man fired first. Judges are on hand to ensure that each contestant did not "jump the signal" and fired with the gun level — as if to hit the other contestant between the head and knees.

At Areadia, California, on 4 June 1972, Bob Munden was timed in a "Walk and Draw" contest at fifteen-hundredths of a second — a world record.

The following year at Norwalk, also in California, on 21 January, Bob claimed another record — this time for "Standing Reaction Blanks".

In this contest a 10.2 centimetre (4 inch) diameter balloon is placed 2.4 metres (8 feet) away from the shooter and is burst by the unburnt gunpowder that comes out of the blank when it is fired. Bob's time for this event was sixteen-hundredths of a second.

But his quickest draw of all is using Self Start Blanks. This is the ultimate test of any fast-gun expert. An electronic clock starts automatically when the firing hand touches the gun. It stops on the noise of the blank.

On 17 August 1968, Bob achieved a time for this draw of just two-hundredths of a second. It was a time that remained unbeaten for nearly eight years. But on 20 May 1976, in an attempt on his own record specifically for *The Record Breakers* who were filming in New York, Bob clocked one-point-six-hundredths of a second — a time that proves he is not only the "fastest gun in the west", but also the fastest gun in the world.

Had he been born a hundred years earlier, Billy the Kid, Wild Bill Hickok and even Wyatt Earp would no doubt have been shaking in their shoes if ever they faced a showdown with Bob Munden — the fastest gun ever.

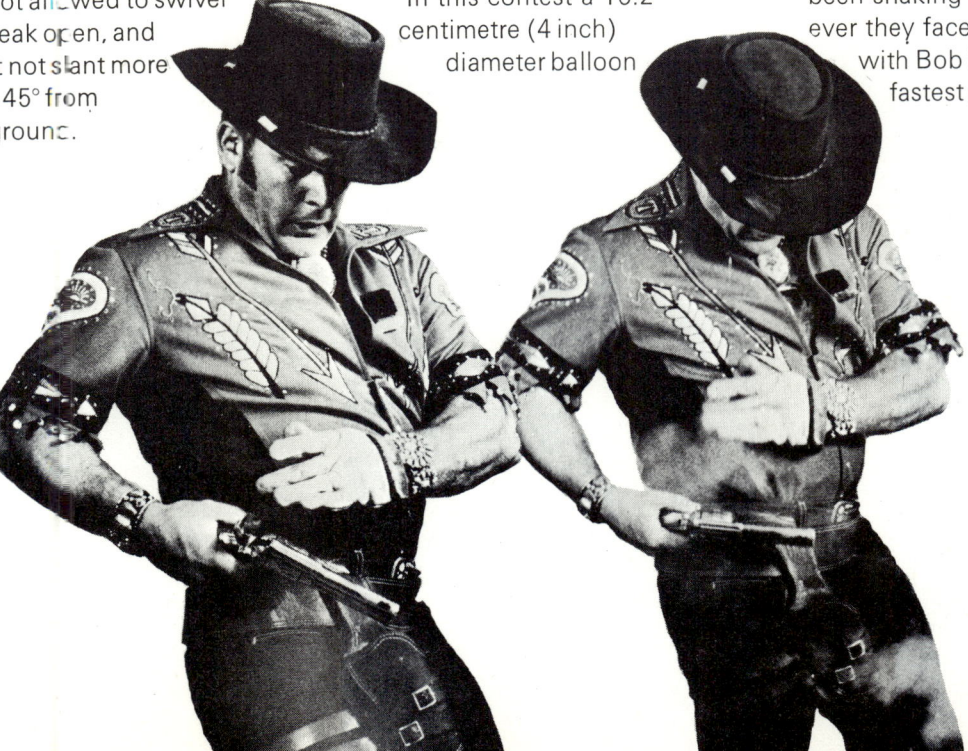

# KNECHT AND KNECHT!

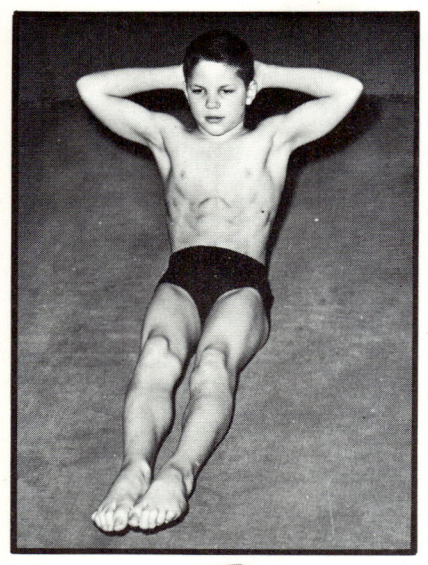

If you want to get fit, try the following exercises:

## 1 Sit-ups

''An exercise in which a person lying flat on the back and with the legs straight, lifts the torso to a sitting position without bending the legs.''

If after a few times you are able to do it quite easily, perhaps you would care to take on Richard John Knecht. At the Idaho Falls High School Gymnasium on 23 December 1972, he performed sit-ups non-stop for eleven hours fourteen minutes – 25,222 of them! During the record attempt, he consumed only honey, orange juice and protein tablets. Richard, incidentally, was only eight years of age at the time.

## 2 Press-ups

''An exercise in which one raises one's body from a prone position to the full extent of the arms and then lowers it, the feet remaining on the ground and the body and legs in a straight line.''

Easy again? Then take on Richard ''Sit-ups'' Knecht's brother – Robert. On 5 February 1976, he performed 7,026 consecutive press-ups in three hours fifty-six minutes. Thirteen-year-old Robert has a tip for anyone who wants to take him on – ''Make sure you do it with your eyes closed. That way the sweat doesn't run into them.''

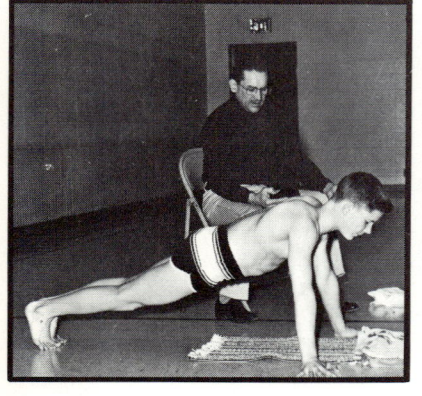

Robert doesn't hold all the press-ups records however. Get your Dad to try these:

### 3 Speed press-ups

Ask him to do as many press-ups as he can in thirty minutes. When he's finished

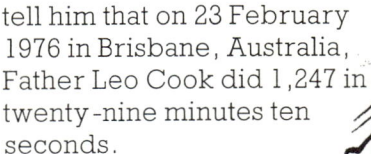

tell him that on 23 February 1976 in Brisbane, Australia, Father Leo Cook did 1,247 in twenty-nine minutes ten seconds.

### 4 Fingertip press-ups

Ask him to do as many press-ups on his fingertips as he can in eighty seconds. When he's finished tell him that on 11 March 1974, James Ullrich of the United States did 140.

### 5 One-arm press-ups

Ask him to do as many press-ups as he can on his right hand. Then ask him to do as many as he can on his left. When he's finished tell him that Henry Marshall of San Antonio, Texas, on 12 September 1975, did 124 one-arm right-hand press-ups in sixty-one seconds and

followed it by doing 103 left-arm ones in sixty-five seconds.

When he's got his breath back, tell him that he's not fit!

And if you think you are, try beating the 45.72 metres (50 yards) dash record set by seventeen-year-old Rick Sorrell of Franklin High School, Ohio, on 1 July 1975. He covered the distance in 24.2 seconds. If you can beat that time you'll be a Record Breaker – but you must do it like Rick did – on his hands!

# WRITING PAPER

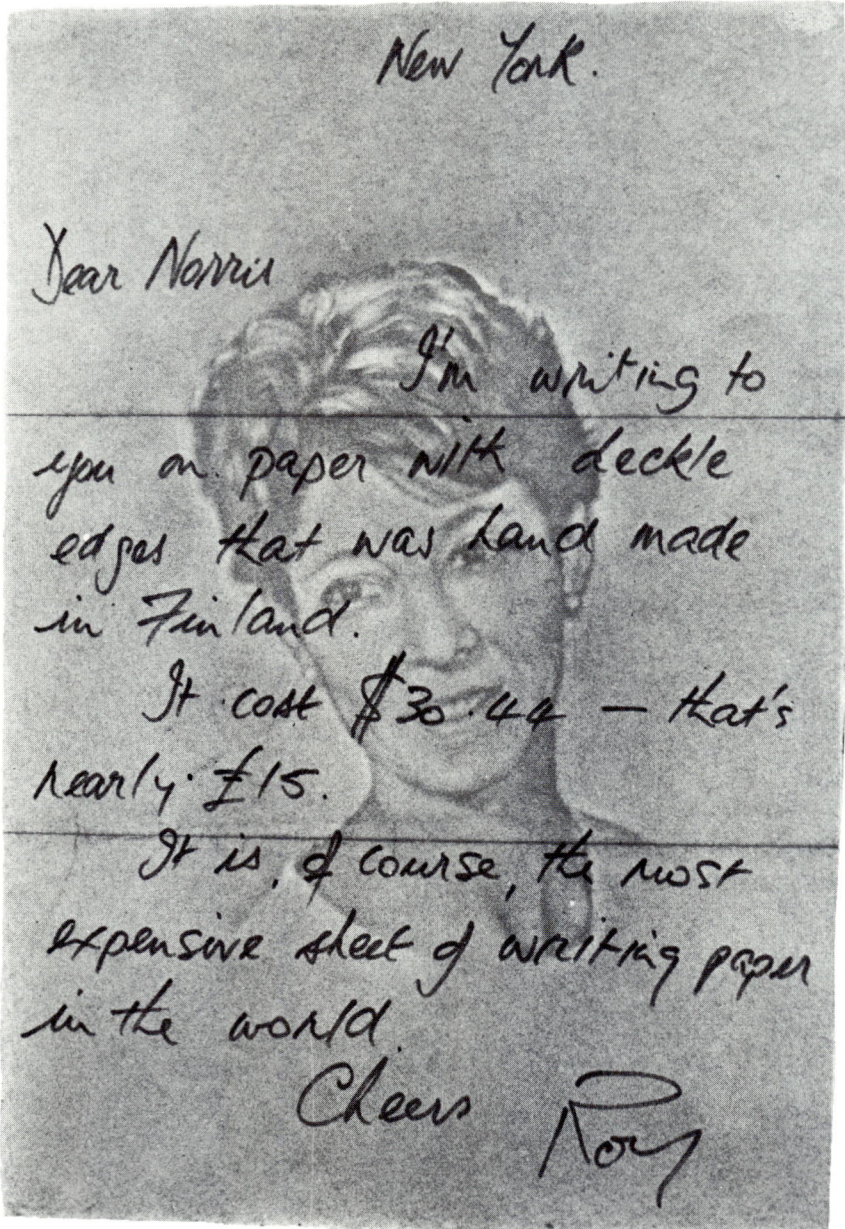

New York.

Dear Norris

I'm writing to you on paper with deckle edges that was hand made in Finland.

It cost $30.44 — that's nearly £15.

It is, of course, the most expensive sheet of writing paper in the world.

Cheers Roy

The most expensive writing paper in the world is that sold by Cartier Incorporated on Fifth Avenue, New York. Hand made in Finland, the buyer can have his or her own portrait or signature watermarked into each sheet. The minimum order is one hundred sheets which today costs $8,000 or £4,520. That's £45.20p per sheet. Envelopes are included.

This sheet, sent by Roy Castle in July 1974, was kindly given to him by Cartiers. He couldn't afford to buy any himself!

# DEATH VALLEY

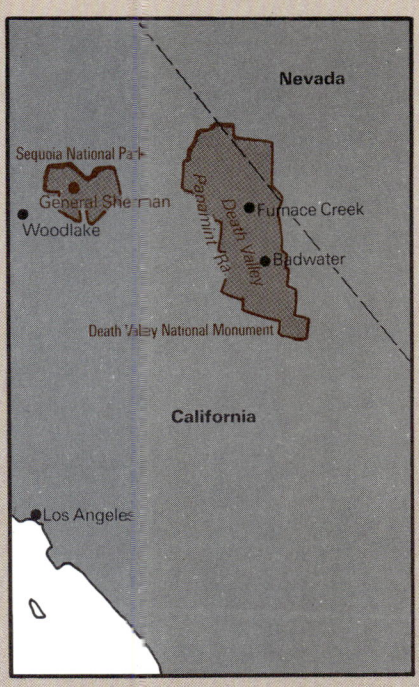

1849 was the year of the Great American Gold rush when thousands of people using covered wagons trekked across America to seek their fortunes in the West.

The first large party to attempt the long and arduous journey travelled in a group of one hundred and seven oxen-pulled wagons, and was led by Captain Jefferson Hunt. They set out from Salt Lake City in Utah on 3 October 1849 to follow the Old Spanish Trail to California. After a few weeks the going became rough, and some people in the party felt Hunt was leading them too far south. The gold fields were not south, but west, and that was the direction they wanted to go.

On 1 November 1849, all but three or four families parted company with Hunt's wagon train and headed due west, putting their faith in a crude map of an old pack-train trail.

This map soon proved to be inaccurate, and most wagons turned back to rejoin Hunt's party. Some, however, with the lure of gold and silver too strong to force them to make any detours, stubbornly continued in a direction they believed to be the shortest route – due west.

They were correct – it was geographically the shortest route. What they didn't know was that it was not going to be the quickest or the easiest.

On Christmas Day 1849 they entered a valley two hundred and twenty-five kilometres (one hundred and forty miles) long and twenty-five kilometres (sixteen miles) wide, the first white people ever to do so. Below them, the floor of the valley – a vast accumulation of salt covering more than five hundred and eighteen square kilometres (two hundred square miles). In front of them, on the other side of the valley, the Panamint Mountains – towering over two miles high. Somehow, someone had to find a way out. Arguments flared among them. With some wanting to try a route to the north, some the south and others convinced there must be a route over or through the mountains, they split into several small groups. Each went their own way – abandoning their wagons when the going became too rough.

One of these groups included three families, those of Asabel Bennett, J. B. Arcane and Henry Wade, together with William Lewis Manly, John Rogers, and Captain Richard Culverwell. Manly and Rogers were two adventurous youths who had joined the Bennetts as drivers in Salt Lake City, and Captain Culverwell was travelling with the Wades. Again and again they tried to escape from the valley floor and failed. With food and water in short supply, they decided they could only possibly survive if they had outside help. Manly and Rogers shouldered packs and set out to climb over the crest of the Panamint Mountains.

Twenty-five days later, they returned from their heroic 644-kilometre (400-mile) venture with the knowledge of a way out and some extra provisions. But the sight they saw on their return was not a pretty one. Approaching the small camp they saw no sign of life – the last oxen having been killed for food and the wagons burnt to make fires.

It was only when they were a hundred metres away that they saw someone attempting to crawl towards them. They'd arrived back from their mercy dash in time – just.

In the twenty-five days they had been away, the Wades, perilously low on food and tired of waiting, had decided to struggle out on their

own. Culverwell, who had no provisions, started with them. When he found that the Wades didn't have enough food for themselves, let alone him, he decided to return to the other two families. He never made it — the only person in the whole of the original group to die in the Valley proper.

As the Bennetts and Arcanes, led by Manly and Rogers, finally staggered out of the valley, one of them turned, looked at the vast salt desert below them and said: "Goodbye Death Valley".

So Death Valley was named. It isn't a surprising name for it either, because many people have died there since that first courageous journey in 1849. And the group of people who made it have ever since been known as the "forty-niners".

The reason for the subsequent deaths in Death Valley is simple. It's hot. It's extremely hot. On 10 July 1913, the World's highest universally recognised temperature was recorded in Death Valley — 134°F (56.7°C) in the shade.

It was for that reason, Alan Russell, the Producer of *The Record Breakers*, decided to visit Death Valley in 1975 to make a film with Roy Castle. Here, he gives his own personal account of what happened.

"You're mad — no one in their right mind goes there in summer."
Those were the first words spoken by Sally Hutchinson of the Southern California Visitors' Council when I told her of our intended filming trip into the heat of Death Valley.

Sally had been helping us to organise all our filming in California, and despite her reservations about our "madness", assisted us in working out the details of how to make a film in the world's hottest place at the hottest time of the year.

As we wanted to film another record breaker — the General Sherman tree in the Sequoia National Park — we worked out a plan to do both in one day. We decided to charter a small plane to fly to Woodlake, a tiny landing strip five hundred and sixty-three kilometres (three hundred and fifty miles) from Los Angeles. There we would collect a car to drive to the Sequoia National Park, film there, and drive back to Woodlake. We would then fly five hundred and seventy-nine kilometres (three hundred and sixty miles) to Furnace Creek in Death Valley, where we would pick up another car and drive to Badwater — at eighty-five point nine metres (two hundred and eighty-two feet) below sea-level, the lowest point in the United States. After filming we would drive back to Furnace Creek and fly the four hundred and eighty-three kilometres (three hundred miles) back to Los Angeles. The one thousand six hundred and twenty-five kilometres (one thousand and ten miles) round trip was to be made in one day — a tight schedule, but possible if all went well.

On 21 August at 8.00 a.m. we met at Orange County Airport, just outside Los Angeles, to put the theoretical plan into operation. Apart from Roy Castle and myself, there were Ray Brislin and Ray Brown — two cameramen, Doug McCash — sound recordist, and Jennifer White — researcher.

The first part of the plan worked well and with the filming of the General Sherman tree successfully completed we started the twenty-five and a half kilometre (sixteen-mile) narrow, twisting, steep descent back to Woodlake. The car was fully loaded with six of us inside and the boot jammed solid with all our heavy equipment. I was driving, and after only two or three miles noticed that the foot brake was becoming weaker and weaker. Soon I was forced to use both hand and foot brakes in order to slow down at the many hairpin bends. When even this had little effect I had no option but to bring the car to a gradual halt. With a sheer drop of six hundred and ten metres (two thousand feet) if the car had left the road it was too dangerous to continue. We were stuck, and there was no alternative but to wait for the brakes to cool down.

By the time we reached our aeroplane it was half-past five – and we were three and a half hours behind schedule. Having eaten a late lunch on board, we touched down on a narrow strip at Furnace Creek an hour later.

The intense heat engulfed us the moment we stepped out of the plane – just in time to watch the sun slowly descend behind the Panamint Mountains, turning the harsh whiteness of the barren salt desert through a new range of subtle tints – each one more mellow than the last.

A decision had to be made whether to fly out immediately or stay and film the following day. Having got this far everyone was reluctant to leave – but where were we to stay ? As far as the eye could see there appeared to be no sign of life. Then our pilot spotted a small wooden shed a few hundred yards away. Inside was a telephone and a list of six numbers, which included one for the Furnace Creek Inn. In no time at all a truck had whisked us to a large, modern, air-conditioned hotel such as one might expect to find in the centre of any great city. In Death Valley it seemed ludicrously out of place. Packed to capacity in winter (the tourist season in the valley) we were the only visitors that night – which was just as well since we only had the dirty, crumpled clothes we stood up in.

After a quick wash – hot water ran out of both taps – a meal in the canteen – cooked by a man who (surprise, surprise) once worked for the BBC in London thirty years ago, we turned in for the night with the temperature outside still over 38°C (100°F).

Early the following morning we met the District Ranger, Dick Rayner, who advised us on how to survive in Death Valley and promised to send help if we had not returned in four hours.

We drove to Badwater and, with a shade temperature of 51°C (124°F) and a sun temperature of about 82°C (180°F), we commenced filming.

While heat waves shimmered over the salt flats which we could hear cracking in the sun, Roy told the story of the Forty-niners' trek and then carried out a few experiments to try and convey how hot Death Valley really is. A candle, removed from a portable ice-box, could be coiled like a spring in less than a minute, and an egg broken into an empty tin lid almost cooked.

Filming in the intense heat presented problems. The equipment was kept out of direct sunlight by using umbrellas and silver heat-reflecting cloths. The film itself was stored in a polystyrene cooling box. But the biggest problem of all was keeping cool ourselves.

Hats were a must, so too were strong shoes – necessary to stop our feet being scorched by the heat of the ground. A heat which at midday was so intense that we were unable to stand still and obliged to shuffle from foot to foot. The temptation was to strip off – a temptation that had to be resisted at all costs.

When the air temperature is higher than normal skin temperature (33.4°C or 92°F), there is only one way to keep cool – by sweating. In Death Valley you don't even know you're doing it, as the sweat

evaporates immediately. Keeping covered helps the body to retain its moisture. Even so, we were each losing two pints of body fluid every hour and had to replace it by drinking an equivalent amount of water.

Failure to do so would have resulted in us being critically ill in five hours and in eight – dead.

The precautions we took paid off – the film and equipment were undamaged and we left safely. With us we took a respect for nature it would be difficult to acquire anywhere else on earth.

It was an experience none of us will ever forget.

Death Valley dustbins – the hottest dustbins in the world!

The author is indebted to the following:
Norris McWhirter, David Hoy and David Roberts of Guinness Superlatives; Jennifer White, Roy Castle, Sheila Elkin and Rachael Hogg

John Cage's music on page 44 copyright © 1962 by Henmar Press Inc, New York, reprint permission granted by the publisher

Photographs on pages 10, 11, Southern California Visitors' Bureau; 14, 15 Bernard Thompson; 18, Central Press Photos; 20, Radio Times (John Marmaras); 22 (bottom), General Electric; 25, the Wadlow family; 26, 27 (inset and bottom), Bermuda News Bureau; 27 (top), Mark Gottlieb; 28, The Press Agency (Yorkshire) Ltd; 29, Central Press Photos; 30, Barnaby's Picture Library; 31, Sport and General; 32 (top), Oxford University Press; 32 (bottom) B. H. Blackwell Ltd, Oxford; 33 (centre), Gleniffer Press; 36 (left), Waseca's Daily Journal (photo by Jo Guck Bailey); 36 (right), Plennie L. Wingo; 37 (left), Associated Press; 37 (right), Harry V. Tipper; 39, 40 (top), Thomson Newspapers Ltd; 40-41, 41 (top), Wally Herbert; 45 (left), Jerry Cammarata; 45 (right), Manchester Evening News; 48, 49, Guinness Superlatives; 50, Joe Davis; 52 (bottom right), Crown Copyright, Science Museum, London; 53 (top left and centre, centre row, bottom left and right), Associated Press; 53 (bottom centre), Danish Embassy; 54, 55, The Waldorf Astoria; 56-57, Associated Press; 58, Keystone Press Agency; 59, Associated Press; 61, Los Angeles Sheriff's Department; 64 (top), Thomson Newspapers Ltd; 65, Radio Times (John Marmaras); 66, Jesse Hart Fosdail; 68 (left), Associated Press; 68 (right), Van Phillips; 69, J. Allan Cash; 70 (bottom), Sartorious Instruments Ltd; 73, Bob Munden; 74, the Knecht family; 75, Guinness Superlatives; 76, Alan Russell; 78-80, Jennifer White

All the remaining illustrations are BBC copyright

Cover photograph by Terry Hardman

Illustrations on pages 50-51 by Malcolm Harrison; 62-63 by Roger Berry; 74-75 and margin illustrations by Paul Cemmick; "Did you know . . ." illustrations by Roy Castle

Designed by Martin Hendry